THE HAPPY PRISONER

UMBERTO SCHRAMM

The Happy Prisoner
Published in 2025 by
Acorn Books
West Wing Studios
Unit 166, The Mall
Luton, LU1 2TL
acornbooks.uk

CONTENTS

ACKNOWLEDGEMENTS

The author wants to acknowledge the difficult and dangerous work that prison officers do every day, as well as the hard work of everyone else involved in the criminal justice system.

He wants to apologise from the bottom of his heart for the terrible mistake he has made and dedicate this book to all victims of crime.

DISCLAIMER

All names of real persons have been changed to protect their identity. Small details of crimes committed and personal characteristics and circumstances have equally been changed so individuals cannot be identified.

Great care was specifically taken that prison officers and individuals working in the prison system cannot be identified. There are no exact dates and the establishments have been given generic names.

PROLOGUE

Whenever I see a prison van I feel a shudder running down my spine.

It's often when I'm cycling through London and have to stop at a red light. As the light turns green the white box overtakes me and disappears into traffic. My mind starts inventing stories. About where it came from and where it is going.

It must be coming from Wandsworth, taking them to any of the prisons outside of London. Or maybe it's coming straight from court, taking them to Pentonville.

I think about the poor guys inside and what they must be going through in this moment. They must be looking out the little window, knowing that they won't be walking those streets for a long time.

In that moment I don't care what they have done; I just know that what they are going through is awful.

The reason I have so much empathy for them is that I was once one of them.

Much of what happened during my three years in prison I will eventually forget, but sitting inside that cubicle looking through the small window at the world outside will stay with me.

It is the strangest feeling.

You look at the world passing by and wonder what it would be like to walk those pavements. What it would be like to walk into a shop. You cannot imagine it.

Like you couldn't imagine what it would be like on a spaceship. You've seen it in movies many times, but it isn't reality.

In that moment, a few years in prison might as well mean forever.

INTRODUCTION

I'm working from home, with BBC Radio 2 playing in the background.

My first job after getting out of prison is in customer service at a flower delivery service. I have to speak to customers who call from Germany, where the company also operates.

Listening to the same complaints all day isn't the most stimulating work, and when I hear that today's topic on Jeremy Vine is the crisis of overcrowding in prisons, I make the spontaneous decision to call in.

This is shortly after Labour's election win. Keir Starmer has inherited a prison system so overcrowded that it now operates an emergency one-in-one-out system.[1]

Every prisoner who gets sentenced in court needs to wait in a police cell until a space in prison becomes available.

I have a lot to say about the subject. Due to my experience of having been in prison I know exactly where the problem lies and how it has become so bad.

Since 1990, the prison population has more than doubled from 40,000 to now nearly 90,000[2], whilst the rate of crime has decreased during the same period.[3] The UK sends more people to prison than any other country in Western Europe.[4]

Recently, 5 climate activists from Just Stop Oil have been handed a combined 21 years in prison for staging a peaceful protest.[5] Wanting to save the world has become an aggravating factor punishable with the longest prison time possible, with defendants being denied the right to explain their actions in court. (A study has found that the UK cracks down on climate protesters harder than any other country in the world).[6] More than 7000 climate activists have been arrested, with more than 120 imprisoned in the UK between 2019 and 2024.[7]

Just weeks later, riots broke out over the stabbing of young girls in Southport, which was wrongly attributed on social media to a Muslim immigrant.[8]

Nearly 500 rioters were jailed,[9] with an average prison sentence of 2 years.[10] The longest sentence was even 9 years.[11] Arguably, these rioters were not criminals, but people who were angry and misinformed, manipulated by social media and high-profile individuals with an agenda. Yes, this was a violent uprising and the state sometimes needs to set an example to deter others. But wouldn't community service, possibly in an Islamic centre to foster dialogue and understanding, have been a much more sensible option for the less serious cases?

I've taken these two examples because they are at both ends of the political spectrum. Whatever your political views are, the fact is that too many people are being sent to prison.

Prison always seems to be the only solution available.

Everything else that might be an option has been put out of use or not properly developed over the last few decades.[12]

In addition to that, sentences have become longer and longer.

This is despite the evidence that increasing sentence length does not work as deterrent.[13] Sentences in the UK have become disproportionately severe – more than twice as long on average as they were just 30 years ago[14], which has led to an explosion in the prison population.

Sending more people to prison for longer does not reduce crime.[15]

In fact it has the potential to increase crime, as rehabilitation in overcrowded prisons at breaking point is impossible, and criminality is rife in prisons that don't work properly.[16]

I want to say exactly that and explain the UK's addiction to prison as the one and only criminal justice solution and the resulting damage to society.

But things don't go according to plan.

I get put through I speak to Tina Daheley, who sits in for Jeremy. She presents me as Umberto from Forest Gate.

(I paraphrase)

"So, Umberto, you have been to prison."

"Yes, for three years from 2020 to 2023."

"And is it ok if I ask you for what?"

This wasn't part of the plan. I wanted to talk about the prison crisis in general, not my offence.

"Causing death by careless driving under the influence of alcohol and drugs."

"Oh..." A pause...

She asks me whether I think my sentence was just. I explain that I am aware of the distress and pain that I have caused.

"Distress and pain." That is the best I could come up with on national radio.

I'm responsible for someone's death and making a whole family suffer for the rest of their lives and the best I can come up with is "distress and pain."

It is such an understatement that I'm ashamed. I have just confirmed the stereotype that offenders don't take responsibility for their actions.

Everything else that I say in the interview does not matter and has lost its meaning.

How dare I talk about prison if I'm part of the problem?

I feel pangs of guilt for the rest of the day. What if any member of the victim family was listening to Radio 2 by chance and had recognised my name? What if that brought it all back up again, brought back the horrendous pain. The last thing I want to do is to open old wounds.

Why did I not think that they might be listening?

I also feel this irrational fear that I might be sent back to prison. Did I violate my license conditions by calling in?

For the rest of the week, whenever I hear a police siren, I think they are coming for me. It is completely irrational, but I cannot shake it off. The fear of having to go back to prison is real.

I have this inner conflict.

On the one hand, I have this desire to tell my story. I want to tell it because – thanks to my experience – I know things about prison that most people don't. I know what's going wrong within the prison system and have ideas how to fix it. And I know how severe the problem is and how much unnecessary damage it causes.

On the other hand, however, I think that I have no right to say anything because of what I have done.

Writing a book entitled "the Happy Prisoner" seems grotesque when the prisoner in question has taken a life. A ridiculous insult. A slap in the face of the victims of crime.

I am part of the problem. Without people like me we wouldn't need prisons at all, so how dare I criticise the system? How dare I say anything at all?

My inner conflict mirrors the one we feel as society when it comes to criminal justice and prison.

Deep down we know what works. We know that if we treat prisoners like animals, we will get animals in return. We will get prisoners that will reoffend after leaving prison because the cause of their offending hasn't been addressed and they haven't received the support they needed. We deep down know that offenders are often troubled people who have had very difficult upbringings, having experienced often horrendous trauma.

We know these things, but they somehow don't sit right with us. They violate our inner sense of moral justice, because we stand with the victims of crime and their suffering.

We want rehabilitation, but offenders also need to be punished. We want both.

And therein lies the problem.

It is what the UK's penal system has been trying to do over the last decades: to rehabilitate and punish at the same time.

And that will never work, because punishment and rehabilitation are the polar opposite, and if you keep punishing someone you will prevent their rehabilitation.

In order for rehabilitation to work, it should be accepted that the deprivation of liberty is sufficient punishment in itself.

It's the harshest punishment in the state's arsenal. Anyone who has ever been to prison will confirm that if you're locked in a 4 m² cell with a complete stranger for 23hours a day, it really does not matter how many TV channels you have.

What happens within prison walls should therefore be focused on rehabilitation, not additional punishment. Only then can prison actually fulfil one of its main purposes, which is to reduce reoffending and ensure there are fewer future victims of crime.

The title of this book – odd as it may be – comes from this inner conflict that I feel about how I should behave considering what I've done, as well as the conflict we feel as society when it comes to how we should treat prisoners.

As much as it goes against our instincts, we need to accept that prisoners need to be to some degree happy for prison to work.

They need to be able to think about a better future for themselves. They need support to address the causes of their offending. They need education and workshops to make up for the basic skills they have never learnt.

They need some sort of perspective. Some light. In their daily routine in prison they need to have a structure that gives them a purpose. They need to know why they are there (Other than just because they are being punished).

At the moment in British prisons, none of that exists. There is an utter lack of any sense of purpose. You are just 'doing time' and wasting away. It's completely pointless.

But much worse than the lack of purpose that I experienced during my time in prison is the current problem of overcrowding and lack of staff.

When a prison is overcrowded, you cannot even dream of thinking about how to reduce reoffending. What you are worried about is that there aren't any riots, any violent attacks on prison officers or between prisoners, or too many cases of self-harm and even suicide.[17] Drug use and criminality are rife, and there's nothing the officers can do to address that in an overcrowded prison. The only thing officers can do is to put out immediate fires. It's horrible and very dangerous for an officer to work in such conditions, which is why understandably nobody wants to do it and there are such staffing issues.[18]

So yes, of course I wasn't happy in prison. And I shouldn't have been because I deserved facing consequences for my actions.

But I did what most other inmates are not able to do: I found some sort of purpose. Goals to achieve within prison walls and a solid daily routine. I managed to reframe prison as an opportunity. It gave me the time to do so many things that I always wanted to do. I had time to educate myself, to read and to write, to learn languages.

As counterintuitive as it may seem, when I was 'happy' in prison, I was open to confront my offending, my flaws in character and work towards change. As soon as I felt I was being punished unfairly, I closed off and became consumed with anger towards the system rather than being able to work on my own flaws. This is what I mean when I say that punishment prevents rehabilitation.

Prison needs to protect society from the most dangerous individuals. It needs to punish those that have done gravely wrong. And it needs to be part of the justice system to work as a deterrent against crime.

But even in prison there are few people so evil they are irredeemable. There has to be some light.

If there is only darkness, there will be darkness forever for everyone.

CHAPTER 1: THE VICTORIAN HELLHOLE
THE DAY OF SENTENCING

When the judge said "take him away" it hit me.

This was it.

Had I at that point asked if I could just nip out for a quick cigarette, the answer would have been a firm no.

Not anymore, and not for some years to come. No more cigarette breaks, no walks to the shop, no pub, no going home in the evenings. The realisation of this was a very strange feeling.

To test if it was really all true, I asked the officer sitting next to me: "Any chance I could just nip out for a quick cigarette before we go downstairs?"

I already knew the answer: a firm, but compassionate NO.

As I was escorted out of the court room I was able to peek over the dividing wall in the middle of the court room behind which the victim's family was sitting.

I saw a woman, maybe the daughter of my victim – we made eye-contact for a split-second, then she looked away embarrassed.

She couldn't look me in the eye.

I had this desire to be able to look her deeply in the eye, so she could see in mine that I was so sorry.

Was this a selfish thought so I could feel better?

I knew that I felt deep remorse about what I had done, but I also knew that ultimately, remorse didn't make much of a difference. It wouldn't change what had happened.

The end result was the same – it might as well have been cold-blooded murder, at least when looking at the consequences.

The officer led me down the back stairs of the court. As we were walking, he was chatting about my sentence as if he'd been discussing the football results. For him this was a normal day like any other.

We arrived at a corridor in the basement with small office cells on both sides.

I was lead into a small office at the very end to the right to wait for my barrister.

As she arrived, we had a brief conversation preparing me for prison, while I was awaiting transport.

Maybe to brighten my spirits, she mentioned all the things I could do in prison. For example, I could meditate.

Wow, meditation, I thought, *do I need to go to prison for that?*

If only I had known at that point how much of a saviour meditation would become for me.

She noted that I hadn't brought anything with me. "I see you haven't packed a prison bag."

INFO: THE PRISON BAG

When you arrive at prison, you will be provided with the essentials such as basic clothing and toiletries. However, it's all very basic.
I would advise you to pack a bag with the most important items, as it will be difficult to send things into prison later on.
Had I known how difficult it would prove to receive sent-in parcels, I would have packed a bag.
Upon arrival at prison all your belongings will be checked.
Allowed items you will be able to keep in your cell.
The items that are not allowed will kept in your stored property until you are released from prison.
In terms of what is allowed and what isn't, think about it in terms of time travel to the year 1997.
Things that existed before then are allowed.
Forget anything that has digital storage or access to the internet. Analogue is fine; digital not.
Some items such as DVD players and DVDs (I told you it was 1997...) will only be allowed once you've reached 'enhanced status'
The following are essential to bring with you:
Cash (this will be transferred to your prison account to buy groceries, make phone calls, order the newspaper, etc. You can keep up to £900 in your prison account. It is absolutely essential that you arrive with some cash.)
2 pairs of shoes: one to wear daily, the other for the gym.
Electric toothbrush or at least a decent toothbrush – the prison ones are not good.

Some books. There will be a library, but you might not be able to access it for the first few weeks. Also they might not have all the titles you want to read.

Writing material: notepad, pens, stamps, envelopes. You can buy these in the prison shop and you also get to send a free weekly pre-stamped letter.

List with all important numbers and addresses. Remember you won't have access to the internet or your phone!

Your musical instrument, if you play. (Guitar is ok; a drum-kit is obviously not...)

A small radio. The radio was one of my most important companions in prison.

If you have the opportunity, pack a good prison bag.

But don't overdo it: remember you'll have to take this stuff with you whenever you change cell or establishment, which will happen all the time.

Be kind to prison staff – prisoners with too much property are a nightmare. If you need another person to help you carry it's way too much.

Think about what you want to do in prison and which items will be most valuable to you.

Regarding clothes: by all means, if it makes you more comfortable, bring some of your own clothes, as long as you don't overdo it.

I personally didn't see the point – it's not like you're going to go on a date or for an important job interview.

The prison-issued sweatpants and sweater worked fine for me.

Your own underwear might be a good idea, actually, as the prison boxer-shorts do get itchy and smell strange when you sweat.

My barrister asked me whether I needed to write down any numbers before they took my phone. She gave me a piece of paper and a pen to write the numbers down from my phone. '*I really could have done this at home*', I was thinking.

Then it was time.

I had been trying to prepare myself mentally as much as I could for this moment. I was led out into the car park where a white prison van was waiting. I stepped onto the van and into the cubicle, being hugely relieved that there was a window so I could look outside.

I don't know why I had been worried there might not be a window, I just remember thinking how unbearable it would have been not to be able to look outside.

Sitting in that cubicle looking outside is one of the strangest memories of the whole prison experience.

You are so glad and relieved to be able to look at the world one last time. Just seeing someone walk his dog on a pavement is suddenly something utterly magical.

At the same time, it is horrendous. You are looking at the streets and the people walking on the pavements, knowing you won't be able to walk these pavements for a long time. In that moment, you are not able to internalise that you won't be in prison forever. It absolutely feels like it will be forever.

INSIDE THE PRISON VAN

Upon arrival at the prison I was placed inside a large holding cell that had a glass wall overlooking the run-down prison reception area. I had to wait for what seemed like ages, with nothing to occupy my mind but my grim thoughts.

Then the door opened and they brought another prisoner in. He had a clear plastic bag with some religious books and some other bits and pieces in it. Rather than sitting down, he started pacing up and down the room. Not frantically, but steadily, like he was on a mission. Up and down. And up and down.

Finally, he leaned against the glass and looked down whilst shaking his head, muttering to himself: "Shit, man! Not this fuckin' shithole again! Fuck!"

As I was sitting there looking at him it overcame me and I started crying.

Rather than showing me sympathy, as you'd maybe expect, he gave me a stern look and said: "Don't do this shit in here, man! People aren't your friends and they'll try to abuse you if they think you're weak." I understood the message immediately, even if I thought he must have been exaggerating.

The door opened and an officer told me to follow him to property handling. There, I was briefly searched and handed over the suit I wore to court, exchanging it for grey prison sweatpants and a jumper. I also handed in my wallet, my phone and my keys.

After having been given a sandwich, kids-size milk carton and breakfast pack we were being lead upstairs to a second holding cell, more filthy even than the previous one, and with misspelled profanities scribbled all over the white, stained walls: 'This place is a shithol!'

I was called into a separate office where I was given a 30sec. induction by an officer assuring me the prison was a safe place and issuing me a prisoner ID card, plus a vape starter pack.

Back in the holding cell, more prisoners had arrived in the meantime.

One fellow prisoner caught my eye as he stumbled in. He was wearing a massive grudge all over his face. As if life had played tricks on him and he was now plotting his revenge. Scruffy and frail-looking, he seemed about 50 years of age and couldn't have weighed more than 50kgs.

As he was moving towards the bench to sit down it became obvious that he was coming down horrendously from a bender – his hands were shaking and his movements at a turtle's pace.

For some reason I knew right there and then that we'd end up sharing a cell. He was struggling to assemble his vape so I gave him a hand. Turned out he was Irish. So Irish, in fact, I couldn't make out a word of what he was saying. His name was Brendan.

I was called in to see the doctor. He asked me when I had my last drink and I told him that morning before court. "The question", he said, "is whether the shaking is due to the alcohol or simply the shock of coming to prison for the first time. If you were still drinking this morning, you'll come off the effects of the alcohol tonight in your cell and might start experiencing withdrawals. I'll therefore prescribe you a course of Librium as a detox."

I was relieved by this – anything to take the edge off was a godsent.

After some more waiting (arrivals at prison and transfers are endlessly long days of waiting and waiting) the moment I had been dreading had arrived – we were lead onto the prison wing.

Walking out onto the wing felt like a surreal, strange dream. Some excitement and curiosity, mixed in with dread. My first thought was: *'my god, this really looks like a prison...'*

We were lead along the landing overlooking the massive 4-level Victorian prison wing, my new cell mate Brendan walking behind me.

WALKING ALONG THE LANDING

INFO: THE LOCAL B-CAT PRISON

Local prisons serve the courts.

Everyone gets sent here first, straight from court, regardless of the type of crime or sentence.[1]

Also, regardless of whether they are sentenced or held on remand (i.e. refused bail) awaiting trial or sentencing.

'Locals' therefore have an odd mixture of basically everyone. Convicted and not convicted: sentenced and not sentenced. The violent murderer could be found in a cell next to the white-collar fraudster. The drug gang lord next to the wrongly charged innocent.

Locals are often crumbling old buildings in city centres that date back to the Victorian era.[2] At that time, prisons operated the 'separate' system in which prisoners were completely isolated and spend the entire sentence in their cells.[3] This means the design of these buildings is completely unsuitable for how prisons are run today.

What's more is that the cells were designed for one person originally, but have now been doubled up, resulting in massive overcrowding.[4]

As an example, Pentonville prison had 550 prisoners when it opened in 1842, today it has nearly 1200.[5]

Due to political failures of recent years, rather than being able to finally close down crumbling and not-fit-for-purpose Victorian prisons, which pose an additional risk to inmates as well as officers, more and more prisoners need to be crammed into them.[6]

We arrived at our cell.

Just the first glance resulted in immediate and profound shock: the cell was filthy and dilapidated beyond imagination.

There was rubbish and dirt all over the floor, the paint was coming off the walls, the furniture falling apart.

I decided to first have a better look inside before I made a definitive commitment, when the metal door behind us immediately shut with a gigantic **BANG!**

The first thing I noticed was that the 'bathroom area' wasn't separated from the rest of the cell, there wasn't even a curtain. And the toilet wasn't a normal white ceramic one but the grey ones you sometimes see in old bus stations or run-down public toilets.

It was basically an enlarged toilet cubicle in a long abandoned bus terminal that someone had also put a bunk bed, a table and a TV in; and that hadn't been cleaned in 30 years.

At that stage I was still green enough to fully convince myself that there must be other toilets on the landing, so you didn't have to do your business right in front of your cellmate.

For some reason, I hadn't actually expected to have a TV in the cell, which was the only positive surprise.

There was no telephone in the cell, so I rang the bell asking an officer to bring me a telephone, as I had to call my parents to say that I was ok. "It's already past lock-up." was his response, not wanting to help me. I had no idea what that meant. After much trying and insisting I convinced him, and managed to call my parents.

Brendan had already claimed the lower bunk, so I climbed onto the top bunk and started reading one of the books I had picked up from the book trolley that we had passed on the landing. It was Carlos Ruiz Zafon's 'The Angel's Game'.

Suddenly, I was getting tired. It had been a long, exceptionally unusual day and the Librium was having effect. Home sweet home. Sort of.

PRISON CELL
FOR TWO INMATES

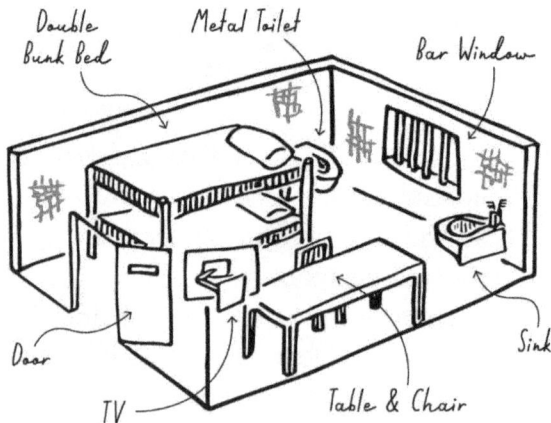

Double Bunk Bed · Metal Toilet · Bar Window · Door · TV · Table & Chair · Sink

CELLMATE # 1: THE CRAZY IRISHMAN

I slept surprisingly well for the first night in prison, although I did have a disturbing dream: I woke up in a completely different cell with 6 other inmates, meaning someone must have moved me overnight.

Dreaming a lot more – or rather, remembering dreams more – is something I noticed a lot during those first few weeks and months.

And I woke up early. "Do you reckon it's morning already?" I asked Brendan. "Oh it's morning alright. You can hear the guards change."

I made a coffee with the little instant coffee sachets we had been given, and the milk.

Then I started jogging on the spot in front of the TV, watching 'Good morning Britain'.

This would become my morning routine for the next few years. The cell was just about big enough, but you had to jog on the spot. Brendan did not seem to mind. He could lie on his bunk and look past me at the TV.

We were locked in all morning, when suddenly the door opened and an officer shouted (For some reason, they always shouted):"S&D!!"

What the hell was S&D?

The door stayed open so I explored the landing, looking for showers and if there was another toilet. As I was standing in front of a locked door with a toilet sign on it an officer yelled at me:

"What are you looking for?"

"I was looking for a toilet."

"These are the staff toilets – you have a toilet in your cell."

I felt the impulse to yell back at him: "But there's someone else in there, for fuck's sake! How am I supposed to do my business in private?"

I explored the landing.

There was the staff toilet, then there was the shower room, consisting of around five or six cubicles that had swinging doors to about chest-height. There was no other toilet for inmates.

In fact, there was nothing but cell doors.

As you reached the end of the landing you reached the main staircase surrounded by a metal cage that had an access door and was locked off.

I was therefore not able to move in between landings and explore the building further. Looking straight ahead you could see into the atrium where all the wings converged.

That was the design of many of the prisons built in the 19th century.[7] very loosely inspired by Jeremy Bentham's panopticon.[8]

There's a round atrium in the middle from which the long wings branch out, similar to the legs of a spider or the spokes of a bicycle wheel.

I don't know what I had been expecting exactly, but I had really hoped there would be a bit more to see. Where was the library? Where was the gym? When would we be able to go outside for fresh air into the yard as you always see in movies?

We were locked back into our cell after less than 30 minutes, and had to stay there for the rest of the day. It didn't matter, as it was just as horrible outside of the cell as it was inside. As a matter of fact, it was better inside the cell.

You had your quiet and could read. Occasionally, an inmate would look through the observation panel in the door and ask for some sugar or a vape capsule.

The door opened again for lunch.

It had to be collect from the servery on the ground floor, then taken back and eaten in our cells. The door which led to the staircase cage at the end of the landing was now open. I followed the other prisoners as they all walked in one direction towards the ground floor, all with their light blue plastic plates and bowls in hand. There were prison officers dotted along the way, sometimes moving prisoners on when they were loitering or having a chat.

The food was ok, pretty much what you were expecting, possibly even a bit better.

There's a big difference between having your first meal in prison and having to eat that same meal 365 days a year.

The food was served by prisoners, one of them was yelling at me because I had some spilled milk on my plate. "What the fuck is this, mate?"

We were also given a breakfast pack for the next day: 189ml milk plus 30g rice pops sealed in plastic.

The second cold meal was brought to all the cells by inmates escorted by an officer via a trolley. It was a small smoked mackerel salad without dressing, crisps and a small chocolate bar. Brendan complained that there was no bread. "How am I supposed to eat this salad without two slices of bread to put it inside?"

This routine would stay the same for the next two weeks. We were locked inside our cell for 23 ½ hrs a day, with less than 30min outside to have a shower. Some days we were even locked in the whole day without the option of a shower.

I did my running on the spot in the mornings, then read all day, and sometimes wrote in my diary. Brendan watched TV all day. Sometimes we chatted a bit, especially when there were political topics to discuss on 'Good morning Britain' or the BBC news. Brendan would mostly watch things such as 'Police Interceptors', 'Border Control' or similar rubbish. In the evenings, we'd often watch a film together.

It became clear that there was no access to the library (but there was a small trolley of books on the landing), gym, education or even access to the prison yard. I hadn't had any fresh air for days.

At that stage, I was still hoping that this would be temporary. My hope was that once the induction period was over, and I'd be moved to a different wing of the prison, the regime would relax significantly. But I would soon realise that the whole prison was under lockdown and that the near-24hr bang-up was the government's response to dealing with the coronavirus epidemic in prisons.

INFO: CORONAVIRUS LOCKDOWN REGIME IN PRISONS

When the full extent of the epidemic became clear, Public Health England advised the government to reduce the additional risk due to overcrowding in prisons by releasing prisoners early and/ or on tag in cases where the end of the sentence was near.[9]

The government rejected this idea ("We cannot lock up literally everyone in the country except prisoners." was more or less health minister Matt Hancock's view, obviously not giving it much thought)[10] and implemented a complete lockdown of prisons, cancelling all activities that involved people mixing (gym, education, mental health support, group work, workshops, vocational training, all work placement that wasn't essential) and locking prisoners behind their cell doors for over 23hrs a day.[11]

This meant for prisoners that all purposeful activity was cancelled and they would spend the whole day in their cells with nothing to do but watch daytime TV. At HMP Wandsworth, for example, the education building was not in use for nearly 2 years.[12]

For fresh air exercise, social and domestics and some essential work, a very restricted regime was introduced that separated prisoners into small cohorts.

Old Victorian prisons with massive wings holding hundreds of prisoners and very little yard space therefore had to run extremely restrictive regimes. More modern prisons with smaller separate buildings and more space surrounding them were able to provide more humane regimes, as populations of prisoners could be more easily isolated whilst still giving them fresh air exercise and time out of cell.

Although there had been an initial plan to release 4,000 prisoners early, only around 350 of those were actually released.[13] The court backlog during the pandemic caused prisoner numbers to fall, and then to swell massively one year after the end of coronavirus lockdowns.[14]

Many other European countries released prisoners due to the risks of overcrowding. France managed to release nearly 10,000 prisoners early without adverse consequences or a public backlash.[15] Turkey released nearly 40% of its 300,000 prisoners, many on house arrest.[16]

It needs to be said that the lockdown worked in the sense that it kept the spread of the virus under control and prevented fatalities, which were relatively low. It also meant that violence in prison decreased massively, simply because everyone was behind their doors the whole day.[17]

It's hard to see how there would have been a different option. Even if many prisoners would have been released on home detention curfew with an ankle tag (and all the resulting difficulties) it would not have solved the fundamental problem that the architecture of most prisons even with lower populations wouldn't have allowed for a safe coronavirus regime, without severely limiting activities.

However, that does not change the fact that for two years, prisoners were denied even their most basic rights with terrible consequences for mental health, rehabilitation and sentence progression.[18]

Over the next few days I slowly learnt how everything works in prison, thanks to veteran Brendan, who had over 40 convictions under his belt and knew the drill.

He showed me how the kiosks – the touchscreens on the landing – worked.

You could sign in with your prisoner ID and manage everything – select your lunch options, order canteen (the prison grocery shop), order a newspaper, or put in 'apps' (applications, for example, to see a doctor).

The canteen is the prison shop run by DHL that allows you order groceries and other necessities, which get delivered to cell doors once a week. The price of items is very similar to a local Londis or Costcutter, and the range similar, if smaller. You can buy sodas and sweets; crisps, fruit and fresh vegetables. Or things like tinned tuna, sardines and beans. Obviously no alcohol or cigarettes, but you can order vapes as well.

If you asked the officers for help or to explain things, they weren't exactly unfriendly, but gave the shortest answer possible.

It became clear quickly that the prison officers simply didn't have the time to explain how things worked. I wondered why there hadn't been an induction or at least an induction booklet to read in your cell. You were just thrown in without any help whatsoever. The reality is probably that in a local hellhole the churn of people walking in and out is so high that it's simply not worth it.

The other thing that was obvious was how many people were still on drugs or coming off them. The constant noise level, especially at night, was incredible. These were druggies going into withdrawal. A constant din of shouting, screaming and banging against cell doors.

At the pharmacy dispense was a daily queue of poor souls waiting for their methadone script. It was a cabinet of horror. Many had scars in their face, missing limbs or a missing eye.

Brendan's confectionary of choice had been crack cocaine. We had some conversations about drugs and alcohol. I mentioned how nasty alcohol withdrawal can be. He said he times when he had delirium tremens, hallucinations and he would see snakes and other animals crawling over the bed. He also confided that he'd been drinking every single day for the past 11 months. I didn't know whether to believe that or not.

Brendan and I did get along. We'd sometimes crack jokes: we were watching 'Field of Dreams' when he remarked that the logline could also apply to prisons. 'Build it and they will come'.

Most of the time, though, I was lying on my bed reading and he was watching TV.

I have to say that I was very lucky to have someone as laid-back and chilled as Brendan as my first cellmate.

Whilst he was cool with me, in interacting with the officers there was a constant quarrelling or trying to obtain something. The first Sunday morning he kept pressing the bell insisting there should be church service, when obviously there wasn't. (and he didn't strike me as the religious type...)

The more I got to know Brendan, however, the clearer it became that he had some very strange attitudes. There was this deeply rooted obsession with money and cheating the system. Along with it came a complete distrust of authorities. They were all bastards and deserved no better than being lied to. He specifically made the point to me that all of his 42 convictions were in England and not a single one in Ireland. "Because the bastards deserved no better!" He hated England and called it the 'cesspit of Europe'

Brendan's sentence was for only two weeks (for some contempt of court issue – I didn't fully understand the whole story).

As his release day came nearer, he was getting agitated and restless, talking non-stop and pacing up and down the cell, also constantly looking through the observation window into the landing. He made me nervous as well.

I was taken aback when he told me about his plans for his release day. He was going to go to Debenhams to steal some jackets and then sell them. Then he was going to retrieve his stash of black label Jack Daniel's bottles and sell them as well (He wouldn't drink them, naturally, as he was "done with that shit")

"Jesus!" I said, "please don't do that, you'll be right back in here!"

"No, no", he countered, "it's easy, and you never get caught."

When the day of his release came, he was more agitated than ever, pressing the bell in the early hours, explaining to the officers that he had to leave early to make the ferry to Ireland today (a complete fabrication, of course).

Before he left later in the morning, he told me about one of his proudest moments.

He was getting released from another prison, apparently escorted out by the governor. As he was out of the gate, he turned around and shouted at him: "I'll keep robbing and pillaging your cesspit of Europe country!"

When he was gone that day I formed an image in my head of what he was going to be up to that day and I had a suspicion that this wouldn't have been his last stint in prison.

What struck as odd was that in the middle of this pandemic someone was given a 2-week sentence. When prisons were already overcrowded and there was a lethal virus out there that was easily transmitted. It didn't make sense to me. What was the point? Looking at Brendan made it obvious to me how pointless short sentences are. Did he learn his lesson from having to be here for two weeks? No of course not, he had done the same thing 42 times before and hadn't learnt anything. Did prison work as deterrent in his case? Obviously not.

Could it be that prison is simply not horrible enough, and therefore doesn't work as deterrent? If British prisons were like concentration camps in which you'd starve to death and die of syphilis, would that teach Brendan a lesson and he'd finally learn the errors of his ways?

I very much doubt that. There is no correlation between how terrible the prisons are in a given country and rates of crime and recidivism.[19] In fact, the countries that have 'holiday camps' as prisons such as Norway have the lowest rates of reoffending,[20] and the countries with the worst prisons tend to have the highest rates of reoffending.[21]

The fact is that Brendan has no intention of going back to prison. Nor did he ever want to go to prison. He simply cannot help himself. He has no concept of how he could live his life differently. The options that could be there in theory simply don't exist to him and he wouldn't even know where to start to change things.

Whatever the solution might be to lead him to the straight and narrow, it's certainly not punishing him, because that has been done 42 times and it didn't work.

INFO: SHORT SENTENCES VS. COMMUNITY ORDERS

Short sentences of less than 12 months are drivers of reoffending and essentially do more harm than good.
In 2023, the Sunak government introduced the 'Sentencing Bill', which asked courts to suspend all sentences of 12 months or less (except in circumstances of immediate risk to an individual). The

government wrote: 'More than half of offenders serving a sentence of less than 12 months go on to commit another crime. For those serving a sentence of six months or less it is 58%.

Meanwhile, for offenders punished with Suspended Sentence Orders with requirements that are served in the community, the reoffending rate is 24%.

The facts are clear – short prison sentences leave offenders in a revolving door of reoffending.'[22]

The law never passed through parliament before the general election of 2024. However, the current Labour government has commissioned an independent review into sentencing. It is led by former justice minister David Gaucke, who has previously expressed wanting to abolish short sentences.[23]

The problem with short sentences is that they offer little rehabilitation but are extremely disruptive to the individual, which increases the risk of further offending.

There simply isn't enough time to attend rehabilitative programs or education.[24] The damage caused by sending someone to prison, on the other hand, is enormous. It will often mean loss of job, loss of home, disruption of family life and social life. Then there are the stigma and difficulty of finding work after release. In addition, prison often acts as a 'school of crime'– the inmate learns from other criminals.[25] Drug use is rife, meaning underlying substance abuse or mental health issues are exacerbated, rather than being treated.[26]

There is also the cost factor – sending someone to prison costs more than £50,000 per year.[27]

Community service costs less than £15,000 per year but has better outcomes in reducing reoffending.[28]

Nevertheless, nearly half of all prison sentences given in 2023 were short sentences of fewer than 12 months.[29]

Meanwhile, the use of community service has been reduced by over 75%, from 200,000 orders in 2011 to around 70,000 in 2023.[30]

I was alone in the cell for less than 30 minutes when a friendly officer came in, gleaming with the fantastic news that a wonderfully clean cell was available for me on B-Wing. This sounded like good news! I even allowed myself to dream: *'oh maybe it's a single cell!'*

In retrospect, my first two weeks in prison can best be described as the 'honeymoon period'. It was horrible, but it was also all new, and I was curious about what was to come. It was the curiosity that made it all a bit more bearable.

CELLMATE # 2: THE OBSESSIVE – COMPULSIVE DRUG DEALER

The honeymoon period ended quickly.

My biggest frustration was that I had hoped the regime would improve and I'd finally be able to access library, gym and have some fresh air. None of this happened – we were still locked in our cell for over 23hrs a day.

The initial impression of my new cell, however, was more than positive. Although it had roughly the same dimensions, everything seemed new and squeaky clean. The walls were white and the furniture functional. There was even a curtain around the toilet area (albeit made of see-through mesh) and the toilet was a white ceramic one.

Z, my new cellmate, seemed a nice enough guy – calm, and mild-mannered. He was reading the prison newspaper as I walked in so we started a conversation about prison in general and our respective sentences. He was short, with short hair and had gold engravings in all of his teeth – a status symbol, obviously. I thought it made him look completely ridiculous.

As ok as Z was, over the next few days I started to struggle with having to live in such close proximity to a complete stranger practically 24 hours a day.

It started with the food. Z didn't close his mouth when he was eating. The noises he was making with the food in his mouth were difficult to tolerate.

All I could think was: "*Please make it stop. Please stop eating. Please be finished*", not being able to blend it out, because we were in such close proximity. I was nailed to a torture bed, forced to endure the noises. It really was the worst kind of torture.

Every evening, he was preparing himself porridge with peanut butter. It smelled nice, but the noise of the soft porridge in his open chewing mouth was inflicting endless pain.

It also soon became clear that the clean cell came with a price. Z had a cleanliness obsession to a pathological degree and was a control freak.

He'd spend half the day washing and cleaning. Every evening he'd spend half an hour rubbing himself with his cream. Then he'd say he's getting acne because he wasn't able to clean himself properly in prison. I thought it was the opposite – he was getting acne because he was cleaning himself too much and getting obsessed. Having a shower took me 5 minutes – he was standing in there for fifteen to twenty minutes.

This wouldn't have been a problem, wouldn't he have started to foist his obsession on me. I had to follow all the rules and face lectures when I wasn't able to live up to his standards.

My bare feet weren't allowed to touch the floor at any point, so I had to slip straight into my flip-flops when I came down from the bunk – a tricky manoeuvre.

Z was using four different cloths for different parts of the sink, which couldn't be cross-contaminated. There was a lot of time spent educating me about the various rules of cleanliness I had to follow; and I usually got things wrong. Reading the TV Guide whilst sitting on the toilet was a big no-no, for example.

Unfortunately, I have to return to the unavoidable subject of the toilet, as I will many times throughout this book.

As mentioned, in this cell, at least there was a privacy curtain (half made of mesh, so you could see through it) Z had bought this 'pooper spray' – an air freshener that I was supposed to use after doing my business.

"Bro, after you shit, use this spray."

Apparently, I couldn't get that right, either.

"Hey bro, thanks for using the spray. I noticed you pressed it three times. It's quite chemical and irritates my nose. Next time, could you please spray it only once. Thanks, bro."

What I found ironic about this was that his own shittiquette was appalling.

When sharing a toilet in a small enclosed space with another person, what you do in order to minimise the smell is to flush immediately as soon as the delivery hits the water. That way, it's flushed away before it has the time to stink up the room. That is common sense. You can really avoid quite a lot of smell if you flush instantly.

He didn't seem to understand or realise that at all, however, letting the smell linger and completely stink up the cell.

Going through my diary from that period, there are pages and pages of moaning how awful prison is. I even decided to change the title of my planned book on prison from : 'The benefits of going to prison' to 'Don't go to prison.'

I was also writing a lot about Z's cleanliness: *'What's the point of having a clean cell in a dump like this? It's like wrapping a turd in cashmere.'*

Psychologically speaking, I was reaching a turning point as the honeymoon period was now over. What had started as a novelty, an adventure, was now my grim and boring everyday reality. It started to feel very difficult.

I needed to distract myself from the terror of sharing a cell and had to think about what I was going to do with my time in prison and what my goals were.

As a starting point, I decided I needed some books. Specifically, language learning books, dictionaries and the complete works of Shakespeare. I also wanted a book on storyboarding because I wanted to learn how to draw storyboards.

My old flatmate Martha had offered to help me in any way needed so I asked her whether she could send me in a parcel.

I found out that due to Covid-19, prisoners weren't allowed to receive personal parcels, but an officer explained to me that someone on the outside could order for me on Amazon and have it sent in.

Martha was happy to go through the order over the phone, which took ages, paying with my debit card which was still saved on the Amazon account.

Unfortunately, my contact with Martha slowly fizzled out after that. We still spoke over the phone one or two more times, but then it became harder and harder to get hold of her.

The phone in your cell only allows you to make outgoing calls to pre-approved numbers. You cannot receive calls, which makes it very frustrating when someone never answers the phone when you call. It's for that reason that I agreed a fixed time to call my mom every week. It just worked best that way, because she knew when I'd call and I knew I'd get hold of her.

Unexpectedly, we had our first gym session.

We were lead through the building by a gym instructor. He led us past the servery towards the far end of the basement. I hadn't been in this corner of the wing before.

He opened the door and led us outside to the yard.

A breeze of fresh air filled my nostrils, immediately refreshing my lungs. It was invigorating, an alien sensation that felt like a gift.

We kept crossing the yard towards the gym. The gym session lasted just under an hour. Z didn't want to go because he wouldn't be able to shower afterwards. It didn't matter anyway, as we wouldn't get another gym session during my time in the hellhole.

As we were coming back from the gym, the instructor locking us back in our cells suddenly had an impassioned outburst about the prisoner two doors down, who had some obvious mental health problems.

"What is he doing here? He needs help! Why do they send him here? Look at him, he needs help!" He mentioned Finland as an example of a country with a better prison system; we talked a little about that and also about Norway as a further example of a better prison system.

Prison gym instructors are at the periphery and therefore good to talk to, as they are not as much burdened and restricted by the staff politics that officer need to follow.

What he said was a reflection of what I had also already noticed. There were many inmates with mental health issues who should be in a mental institution and not in prison. They simply shouldn't have been here.

Just a day before, for example, some guy had walked into the servery at lunchtime with his bed sheets under his arms, looking confused.

After nearly two weeks of having been locked in our cells without any fresh air whatsoever (apart from the brief walk to the gym), we finally managed to see more of the prison yard for fresh-air exercise.

25 minutes of walking in a circle (exactly like you've seen it in movies) in a tiny concrete yard that was wedged in between two tall prison wings. There was a massive heap of rubbish in a corner. It was a depressing affair.

EXERCISE FOR 20 MIN.

Daily life in the cell with Z was grinding me down more and more.

It was clear to me that his cleanliness obsession was a coping strategy. He'd lost control over his life, so this gave him the illusion of retaining some of it.

His big problem was that he'd been in limbo for the last 6 months.

Z had been arrested and charged, but his trial was still months away. He was kept in prison 'on remand', essentially 'parked' until his trial would start. The reason people are held on remand is that releasing them home on bail until the start of their trial is considered too risky. They might pose an immediate danger to others (or themselves) or they might be a flight risk. In the case of drug dealers such as Z it is often because they'd be able to continue their criminal activity from home.

He was arrested when he drove a customer to a nearest tube station. After the customer got out of the car and walked towards the tube he was approached by the police. Presumably, this was because Z's car was already on the police's radar, and they'd be following him. It's the best explanation of why someone stepping out of a car would suddenly be approached by the police for no apparent reason. What the customer then did, because he got scared, was immediately admit everything and point towards the car. Z was stopped and arrested. (As I've learned during my time in prison, these accounts need to be taken with a pinch of salt. There is often vital information missing, and defendants make themselves look less culpable than they actually are. Mostly, that is, not always.)

Z was struggling to deal with the uncertainty of what was going to happen to him. He held a grudge against the person who grassed him up and hadn't really processed the situation that he found himself in. In his head, he was still living 'at home', rather than accepting that he'll spend quite a while in prison and deal with it mentally. This could be seen when he was on the phone to his partner for hours every single evening. Keeping in touch with loved ones is positive of course, but this was extreme and struck me as not healthy. He also had a very young child and his girlfriend was pregnant, which made the situation all the more difficult.

Regarding the sentence that he was likely to receive, he was very unrealistic, expecting maybe a year or so, when it was clear to me that he'd be getting a lot more. They had found drugs in his home, as well as £70k in cash. He had hidden all of that money and the drug dealing from his girlfriend – I had no idea how that would even be possible.

Some might disagree with me on this, but I didn't see the reason why he had to be held on remand, especially considering the pandemic. He could have received an ankle-tag to stay at home during certain hours until his trial would start. That would have given him the opportunity to stay with his family and to prepare for his time in prison. From everything Z told me and also from the vibe that he gave off, it was obvious to me that he wasn't a large drug kingpin. He was a small dealer who sold some cannabis and some coke, nothing worse than that. He didn't carry a gun nor has he ever physically harmed anyone.

My opinion is that remand should be reserved to those who pose an immediate physical danger to others, and therefore need to be kept behind bars to protect their potential victims. Yes, Z was a drug dealer, but so are thousands others and that number isn't going to change regardless of how many are put behind bars. As soon as one drug dealer is behind bars, someone else will have immediately taken their place.

Yes, remand time counts towards your prison time, but the problem with it is that as you haven't been sentenced, you also cannot receive a sentencing plan that would offer you to attend education or offending programs.

In theory, remand prisoners should have many privileges, as they haven't been convicted of anything yet and in the eyes of law are still innocent. In practice, however, remand prisoners have fewer privileges as they cannot participate in most prison programs. They are just wasting away in limbo, doing nothing, often for months or even years. And during this time they will stay at the local hellhole, whilst convicted prisoners will be swiftly transferred to the appropriate training prison or even open prison, if they are very low risk.

As a consequence, local prisons are completely clogged up with remand prisoners.

INFO: REMAND – WHEN THE INNOCENT ARE BEHIND BARS

Apart from the issues mentioned above, holding prisoners on remand also carries with it a much more sinister problem: That many are wrongfully imprisoned. Not everyone who is charged with a crime will actually be found guilty of that crime. In addition, not every convicted crime carries a custodial sentence. Many remand prisoners – once their cases are processed in court – are acquitted, receive a non-custodial sentence or a suspended sentence.

As there is a huge court backlog of over 70,000 cases, many are held on remand for months or even years before their case is heard in court.[31]

There are currently 17,000 remand prisoners, which is nearly 20% of the prison population.[32] This demonstrates how much remand affects prison overcrowding.

Around 20% to 25% of them will not receive a custodial sentence.[33] This means that out of the 17,000 currently held on remand, at least 3,400 are wrongfully imprisoned; some of them for months or even years.

Only 44% of remand prisoners are held for violent offences.[34] This leaves over 50% that do not pose an immediate physical threat to others.

The backlog in court is so immense that it has led to the grotesque situation where lawyers advise their clients to plead guilty and avoid a trial, just to be able to be released from prison.[35] Many have spent such a long time in prison already, that even if they plead guilty and receive a custodial sentence, they will be immediately released.

Being imprisoned has devastating consequences. It will lead to loss of job, loss of relationships and friendships, possibly loss of family and home; plus the negative mental and physical health consequences as well as the stigma attached to it.

There is no question that in many cases there is no choice but to hold someone on remand. If an offender poses an immediate threat to others, they need to be kept behind bars.

But remand as it is used at the moment is not restricted to those individuals. It is used much wider, leading to unnecessary prison overcrowding and the imprisonment and destruction of livelihoods of too many that are innocent or have committed minor crimes.

My encounter with Z made me think of the coping strategies we adopt when we are faced with imprisonment.

He was clearly in complete denial regarding his situation, to which the fact that he was held on remand for so long contributed. Due to the intimacy of the cell I had no choice but to listen in to his long phone conversations with his partner.

Z had left school when he was 13, was therefore lacking basic education that could provide him with employment other than drug dealing, which is the only thing he knew. And he didn't see how he could provide for his family without the income drug dealing provided.

We spoke about this and I told him that prison should be the opportunity for him to learn something that would help him get out of that situation. Finish his schooling and maybe learn a trade. But did these opportunities actually exist? They certainly didn't at the local hellhole, at least not while in complete Covid-19 lockdown. And they most definitely didn't for remand prisoners.

Z eventually decided that he wanted to work on the wing to occupy his time, a positive development. For the few jobs that were available (cleaner, kitchen worker) you had to have your cell on the basement floor, so he asked to be moved.

Once again, I allowed myself to dream that I'd now have the cell to my own, even if it was just for a day or two. I needed some time by myself, some privacy – a small break to recharge the batteries.

It was a complete pipe dream.

This time it did not take 3 minutes for an officer with a clipboard to stand at the cell door, asking me to move cell as well.

It was astonishing. The amount of times I had asked every single officer on the wing for a replacement of my old, wafer-thin broken madness that made my back hurt: no chance.

I didn't have a chair so I had to eat my food standing up as I couldn't sit on Z's bed. One officer was really helpful and we walked through the entire wing, trying to find a spare chair. There simply wasn't one. And there apparently wasn't any kind of storage where spare items would be kept, either.

It was not possible to get a chair, it was not possible to get a mattress, no matter how many hundreds of times you asked.

But if a bed was empty it would be filled within 2 minutes.

CELLMATE #3: THE CELL-SMASHER

The smell of burnt paper. I didn't at first realise the smell similar to burnt paper was actually burnt paper. That's how you smoked the Spice. You modified the vape pen, using the battery to burn a piece of paper that had been drenched in chemicals. Then you smoked the burning paper.

As I was on the top bunk I didn't see what was actually going on underneath me, I only noticed the smell.

My new cell was a dark dungeon on the basement floor. It really was a dungeon, there was no natural light coming in whatsoever. The entire wall plastered with cutouts of page 3 models.

My new cellmate Jason was super hyper in the mornings – when he received his daily dose of speed – and sleepy in the evenings when he started smoking Spice.

The speed was actually his ADHD medication in capsule form. He took it back to his cell (having pretended to swallow it at the pharmacy counter), opened the capsule, separated the brown powder from the white one. He then discarded the brown bit and sniffed the white stuff. "Just like speed", apparently.

To the complete smashing up of our cell there had been an immediate catalyst and an underlying smouldering frustration. The frustration was that Jason wanted to use the kiosk on the landing to send an important message to Offender Management. As we were in full lockdown, we were not allowed out of our cell and on the landing, meaning you couldn't access the kiosks. That was a problem and didn't make sense, because you needed the kiosks to do absolutely everything.

He had early in the morning explained the situation politely to an officer and asked if he could please briefly use the kiosk. The officer assured him that it would be possible later in the day, just not now.

As the day progressed he received this same message from the officer again and again. Yes, later, just not now.

When the day was nearing to its close, he eventually became slightly annoyed and snapped at the officer.

"Now you won't get it at all!" was the officer's reply and then slammed the cell door in his face. That was the catalyst.

It all happened fairly quickly and all I was able to do – sitting on the top bunk watching what was happening – was to say: "Don't do this, man!" I repeated the same thing about ten times like an idiot. "Don't do this, man!"

When he was finished, most of the furniture of the cell had been smashed to pieces. The bed and the cupboard were solid enough, but table and chair were gone.

He had also smashed the glass of the observation window with a leg of the table, sending shards all over the floor.

After he had it all out of him he sat on the bed, now calmer. He had been on autopilot. The costs of the damage would be added to the £3000 he already owed the prison service. His debt meant that he wasn't allowed to order canteen, leading to additional problems, as he had to buy his vapes on the black market at inflated prices.

There is such a thing as personal responsibility. But there's also the fact that in prison you are not dealing with a slice of the general population. You're dealing with a population that is vulnerable, angry, damaged and has special needs. It needs more support.

The incident was completely avoidable. It would not have happened in a prison with adequate staffing levels and a reasonable regime that, for example, allowed the kiosks (which are needed by prisoners for absolutely everything) to be used regularly.

Several cells were already completely smashed up and rendered unusable because people had destroyed the sink, leading to flooding. And here we're only talking about property damage. How many incidents of violence, either among prisoners or between officer and prisoner, are the results of built-up frustrations stemming from an understaffed, underfunded and overcrowded system?

And what is the impact on the mental health of prisoners?

INFO: MENTAL HEALTH – A KNOWN UNKNOWN

There is no clear data on how many prisoners have mental health issues.

A report by the House of Commons Justice Committee (2021–22) found that 'there is no clear picture on the extent or nature of mental health problems in prison, nor how much is spent on treatment and whether the money is well spent.'[36]

The Ministry of Justice admits: 'we do not have a complete understanding of the overall prevalence of mental health needs of prisoners, due to the cessation of NHS health and justice indicators of performance.'[37]

The data that exists is based on surveys relying on self-reports, as well as the information prisoners report to prison inspectors, which are published in the annual reports of the Prison Inspectorate.

Whilst every prisoner gets screened for mental health problems on arrival at prison, there is no centralised IT system that collates and shares the results of these screenings. In addition, arrivals at prison are often hasty and prisoners are likely to underreport problems as they want to get the screening done with. Later on, prisoners are likely to underreport problems due to perceived stigma, distrust of authorities and because they might not be able to recognise mental health issues.

What is clear from the existing data, not surprisingly, is that prisoners have much higher levels of mental health problems than the general population.

The Inspectorate of Prisons survey carried out in 2023 showed that 59% of men in prison reported a mental health problem.[38]

The Centre for Mental Health found that 9 out of 10 prisoners had at least some mental health or substance abuse issue in a 2024 study.[39]

The estimates on specific mental issues vary, but just to give an example: the prevalence of ADHD amongst prisoners is around 25%, compared to 4% in the general population.[40]

It is estimated that over 50% of prisoners have some form of personality disorder, compared to around 10% in the general population.[41]

At least 40% of prisoners suffer from depression and/or anxiety.[42]

The rate of self-harm has been increasing, with 13,640 prisoners self-harming in the year '23/'24 (over 15% of the prison population) and 3,349 incidents of self-harm requiring hospitalisation.[43]

The number of suicides in prison has stayed stable (with a spike during the pandemic): 85 cases between March '23 and March '24. 21% of men in prison have attempted suicide at some point in their lives, compared to 6% of the general population.[44]

CELLMATE #4: THE SNORER

There was clearly something wrong with Luke. What exactly that was, however, was a bit more difficult to tell. He had a wonky eye, which gave him a slightly grotesque appearance. It made him look a lot more hostile than he actually was, and a lot less intelligent.

It was obvious that he was an intelligent guy. He'd done a criminology degree in prison via the Open University. He was also learning Russian vocabulary in our cell. We had some interesting and constructive conversations, especially about the prison system. I learned a lot about the recent history of prisons in the UK from him.

This coincided with me educating myself on the prison system and the history of imprisonment in general. I started reading the prison newspaper 'Inside Time' every month and started hearing for the first time about things such as the Strangeways Riots of 1990.

I wrote a letter to the prisoner governor with 6 specific points of how to improve the prison. One point was the dreaded 'breakfast packs' which were an unbelievable waste of plastic. A tiny 30g bag of cereal in plastic was then surrounded by another plastic bag that contained tea and sugar sachets. I suggested it should be replaced with a weekly ration of oats in a paper bag and a weekly box of tea of coffee, saving all the plastic packaging.

Another was that, as the library was closed, there should at least have been the possibility of ordering books using a form. A few weeks later, I did actually receive a 'library book order form'. Whether it was my suggestion that was implemented or sheer coincidence, I do not know.

Luke was also a much nicer guy than he appeared to be from initial impression. He often lent me his vape for a few 'blasts' when mine had run out just before canteen day.

This was a constant occurrence. It happened pretty much every week. It happened to other prisoners as well, so there was a black market of vapes to be sold at double the price just before canteen days. Payment would be via bank transfer or other canteen items.

The problem was that I didn't just need money for the vapes (which were £3 for a pack of 3 ; and I needed about 4-5 packs a week, but often bought just 3, stupidly thinking that I'd manage with less that week), but also for phone calls and, most importantly, for food.

The food provided was simply not enough to get by.

My mom was in the process of getting a credit card, as it was the only way to send in money, and she didn't have one. The debit cards we use in the UK didn't then really exist in Germany. What is used instead are so-called EC Cards, but those weren't accepted. (They are now.)

She had asked a friend who owned a credit card to transfer me money a few time, which was kind of both. My friends Adam and Guy were also both so kind to send me some money. And Hannah, a friend and co-worker had actually sent me 50 quid.

Still, there was never enough. I was cursing the fact that I hadn't arrived with more cash in my wallet!

A few hundred quid would have completely sorted me out for the first few weeks and months, if only I'd known. But obviously I didn't know about the prisoner money account and I thought the money would just be left in storage until release. I also obviously didn't know that the food given would be so shockingly little and not nearly enough to get by.

Luke had a similar problem. He was calling his brother several times asking for some help and left a very angry voicemail, when the brother just wouldn't answer. Although I suspected that his need for money didn't just stem from the need for food, vapes and phone calls.

I realised that he was also smoking Spice. I could immediately recognise the smell by now. Although he was much more discreet about it than Jason, and wouldn't pass out in the evenings, it was still obvious.

In regards to his brother I told him that I had a similar situation with Martha, my flatmate who had promised to help me and was now letting me down, explaining that it'd be more and more difficult to get hold of her.

"In prison you find out who your real friends are," he told me.

A statement that is both a cliché, but also true.

Luke had originally been in prison for a robbery gone wrong (wrong as in he got caught, not that people died) to fund his drug habit. His sentence had been 11 years.

He did his time, seemingly with success, graduating from an Open University degree in criminology. He was released on licence and for the first few years everything went well. He was clean and sober, went to NA meetings and had full-time employment. Then the pandemic hit and he fell off the wagon. He had to have an operation for a heart condition and after the operation released himself from hospital on several occasions, without permission, to score drugs, which lead to his recall to prison

INFO: RECALL

When you are released from prison, you are released 'on license', meaning you will have to adhere to license conditions for a fixed period of time. These can include attending probation appointments, staying at a fixed address, informing probation of important life changes, not taking drugs or drinking alcohol, and obviously not reoffending. If you break the conditions of your license, you can be sent back to prison. This is called 'recall'.

The purpose of the license is to mitigate the risk of further offending whilst the offender is adjusting to life on the outside. If an offender fails to stay in contact with probation or misses appointments, his risk has increased and probation might decide to recall him to prison. The duration of the license period depends on the sentence. In determinate sentences it is 50% of the sentence length. To give my case as example: I was sentenced to 6 years, 3 of which I had to serve in prison, the other 3 on license. I am currently still on license, meaning I could be sent back to prison at anytime to serve the rest of my sentence, should I mess up.

There are currently over 12,000 individuals in prison that have been recalled – 15 % of the prison population.[45] The number is the highest it has ever been. In contrast, in the 1990s, the number was fewer than 150![46]

The main reason for the enormous increase is a change in law that gave probation alone the power to recall someone without needing a court's approval.[47] In addition, increases in sentence lengths and resulting increases in license periods mean probation have ever higher workloads with more offenders on license.

The Prison Advice and Care Trust found that between April and June 2024, for every 100 prisoner released, 77 were recalled.[48]

Around 75% of all recalls were for non-compliance, and only around 25% for actually committing another offence. 36% of recalls were for failure to stay in touch with probation and 23% for being homeless.[49]

The PACT writes: 'too often people are being recalled on minor technicalities or because they don't have the support they need – they may have missed and appointment or have nowhere to live. We should consider returning to a system that required a court to recall someone to prison rather than an overworked probation officer.'[50]

Offenders on license live in constant fear of being recalled to prison. According to Martin Jones, Chief Inspector of Probation, this leads to a 'lack of trust', which in turn actually increases the risk as offenders are afraid to have an open conversation with probation.[51] Offenders have to be very careful what to tell probation, as everything could be interpreted as a risk factor that warrants a recall. This includes seeking help for mental health issues or a substance abuse problem. It has therefore become a system that often works against people, rather than with them.

It is of course a balancing act for probation officers. The consequences of missing warning signs could be disastrous – many of the offenders on license have committed violent crimes. There is a fear that a further crime committed by someone on license could make the news headlines, which results in a tendency to prefer to err on the side of caution. It's a risk-averse blame culture that means too many offenders are recalled.[52]

The problem I had with my workout routine was that whereas I could train my chest doing push-ups on the floor of the cell, there was nowhere I could train my back.

Fortunately, we were on the ground floor of the wing and I found some beams running overhead along the width of the landing that I could use for pull-ups. It was a temporary solution, because a female officer soon came to me:

"No exercising on the wing."

"Understood. But where am I supposed to exercise? It's really important for my mental and physical health" I asked her, slightly irritated that everything was made so difficult.

"The gym."

"The gym is closed because of Covid."

"No, it's open, I saw them take a group down there earlier."

I couldn't believe that an officer working here would be ignorant about the regime the prison was actually running. And also that she wouldn't care about the importance of exercise.

I had to find another solution because I didn't want to get into trouble. I had this idea of using the bed-frame of the top-bunk and a sheet of bedding to do some sort of rowing pull-up that would train my back and biceps. The problem was that this exercise would make the entire bed shake when Luke was still in bed sleeping.

He usually slept until 10.30am every day. *Who can sleep until 10.30 when they're in prison?*

I couldn't help it, I had to do it anyway. I attached the sheet to the top of the bunk on my side, furthest away from Luke as possible and started lifting myself up. I did a set, rested for a while, and then did another.

He kept pretending to sleep for a while, then, all of a sudden started losing it completely.

"Are you taking the piss? Enough! There are fuckin' boundaries! This is my bed. I'm trying to sleep here! You've got three years to get fit! Three years!"

I have to admit that he had a point. I myself was hyper-conscious about personal space, it felt hypocritical of me. At the same time, what could I do if there was nowhere where I could train my back? I had to try to improvise and find solutions. The bedframe was off-limits now, so I kept on searching for a different solution.

The human snore is not a pleasant sound at all. Being forced to listen to it was one more form of torture.

Even though Luke told me that I was the first cellmate he ever had who didn't snore, I couldn't say the same thing about him.

This was the first time in prison that I actually couldn't sleep.

As I was lying there, the picture that formed in my head was that of Jabba the Hut sucking in air with his giant fat flabby mouth.

I felt sorry for millions of married women who had to endure this. The problem was that, if the snorer is your partner or a friend, you can gentle move them in a different position, or even wake them up and tell them they're snoring. Or you can simply sleep in a different room. Here, however, once again, you were trapped and had to endure the torture.

It was so intolerable; I somehow had to try to move him. Considering how he was sometimes kicking off when I was invading his space, this was a problem. I needed to find some kind of long object to slightly poke him and make him turn. The best thing I could find in our cell was a large hardback book.

When it did work and he actually turned, it was only quiet for about a few seconds. Then he started snoring again. I had to try it again, praying that he wouldn't wake and I'd have to explain what I was doing.

I also tried to find something that I could stuff my ears with to block out the noise, but there just wasn't anything suitable. I tried paper, but that wouldn't seal it my ear properly and started to hurt after a while. They did actually sell earplugs on the canteen, but that didn't help me the moment I didn't have any. Pushing my pillow against my ears didn't help either...Nothing helped, it was a nightmare.

Better than the nights were the days. (After 10.30am that is, when Luke was up...)

We talked about the prison system. As he'd been around for a while, he was able tell me how things used to be in the old days.

Apparently, there was an enormous amount of officer violence towards prisoners up until the late 90's. Prisoners were regularly beaten up.[53]

Cells did not have a toilet but a bucket in the corner, sometimes for three prisoners who would share a cell. That bucket had to be 'slopped out' into a sink on the landing in the morning, which was often blocked. The whole wing stank of shit and piss.[54]

The Strangeways riot of 1990 – where prisoners went on the roof of Manchester prison to complain about the squalid conditions, causing a national scandal and millions of damages – had a major impact on getting toilets installed in all prison cells in the 1990s.[55]

I couldn't believe it when I heard about the toilets. We were not talking about the 1890s, we were talking about the 1990s. Unbelievable and disgraceful for a country that considers itself a world leader and a model on human rights. In fact, Victorian prisons had some sanitation installed in cells as early as 1859. These were later taken out, either because they didn't work properly or space needed to be made to turn single cells into doubles and even triples.[56]

Luke told me that he was going to move cells, because his uncle had just arrived on the wing and he wanted to share the cell with him. (Would you want to share a prison cell with your uncle? I'm really not someone who can judge, but if a family has more than one member in prison...).

As before, within minutes after Luke's departure, the clipboard officer stood at the door, moving me as well.

CELLMATE #5: THE LATVIAN VODKA MAKER

"Hey student!"

If I was a student at the school of prison, in Vlad I had found my teacher who knew everything. At least that's what he was convinced of. He was a real man – a wise teacher – and I was a student who had much to learn.

We got off to a difficult start, however, as he downright refused to share a cell with me. I had to call an officer to mediate and resolve the issue.

The officer grotesquely explained to me: "You have the right to a bed in this cell. It is your right to stay in here." I thought this was a strange statement. Wouldn't having a right imply that there was a choice? As always I just nodded and refrained from making any snarky comments.

Things between Vlad and I didn't get much better when I refused his welcome shot of self-made vodka.

"In Latvia", he explained "when we meet new people we drink. If not, heavy insult. Heavy insult, not nice."

"Under normal circumstances, on the outside, I'd gladly drink with you." I told him, "but these aren't normal circumstances, you must understand. If we ever see each other on the outside, I'll share a drink with you."

He wasn't convinced.

Next, he proceeded to show me a piece of paper that I supposed had Spice on it.

"You smoke, I smoke", he offered.

I realised this wasn't going to be easy...

Vlad was a colossal pain in the ass.

He just wouldn't leave me alone and let me do my thing. If I was reading a book lying on the bed he would constantly stick his head into the book or try to engage me in conversation. But conversations weren't really possible because his English was so poor.

Vlad had a huge physical presence. He was tall, muscular and a little frightening. But it soon became clear that behind his big physicality and his show of bravado was a child that craved attention. I saw his fragile side when he was drunk and showed me some pictures of his partner and newly born son. I just felt so sorry for him. Whatever someone did to end up in prison, it's hard not to have sympathy for them and the devastating impact that incarceration has on their family.

Vlad's mornings were spent recovering from last night, drinking more vodka and waiting for the door to open so he could peddle his product, 'do business' as he called it.

When there was outdoor exercise, he tried making deals with everyone. He was also pissed half of the time and there was no way the officers didn't notice that. Mostly, they just tolerated it. They did, however, take away our self-made (using 2l water bottles strung together by bed-sheets) weights as they posed a security risk.

I had a conversation with an officer about this, arguing that the rule made no sense, as we had much more dangerous objects in our cells. Our chairs had sharp ends, whereas the self-made weights were completely blunt. The officer sort-of agreed, but also didn't. That was always the case. If there was a rule it was better not to think too much about whether it made sense or not.

After lunch, Vlad would usually start smoking Spice. This made him childish and silly. He would sing, utter strange expressions, continually annoy me and prevent me from doing anything other than giving him attention.

After a while, he would get the munchies and eat mountains of food in three different places, all whilst tumbling around the cell smashing into everything. This was made worse by his size. Everything would be shaking, like in an elephant stampede. Eventually, he would fall asleep.

He woke up early evening and started preparations to make his vodka product, which was an elaborate process.

The TV was on all day and night, and whenever I tried to put on the news or something informative, he switched it back immediately to some rubbish reality show.

The only time I was able to do anything, and was not constantly harassed, was when he was asleep.

INFO BOX: HOW TO DISTILL VODKA IN A PRISON CELL

You start with a mixture to make normal hooch. For this you only need a plastic bag that you can seal and the starter.

This needs to be something like marmite. You then need lots of sugar and foodstuffs that can ferment. Vlad used tinned tomatoes, bread, lots of sugar, and some other half mouldy vegetables, that he kept in a container. Others use oranges, which is why they're often not allowed in prison around Christmas, along with sugar and marmite.

The bag then needs to be hidden somewhere, in a closet or under the bed. The closed bag will fill with air as the mixture ferments, therefore needs to be opened every few hours to release the air, along with a terrible stench.

Whenever Vlad woke up in the mornings, the first thing he did was tend to his bags. It always seemed to me like he was looking after his children.

After 4-5 days the hooch mix is ready for the next process, the distillation.

For this, a lot of paraphernalia was needed.

The heating element of a prison-issue kettle would be used to boil the hooch inside a plastic bucket.

A soap tray was suspended in the middle of the bucket. The very top was sealed off with clear foil which was covered with water.

As the steam of the boiling hooch condensed at the top, it would after a while form drops that would drip into the soap tray in the middle. The tray had a small tube connected through a hole, connecting a small bottle outside the bucket that would slowly fill with the distilled hooch. The smell was obnoxious.

DISTILLING VODKA IN A PRISON CELL

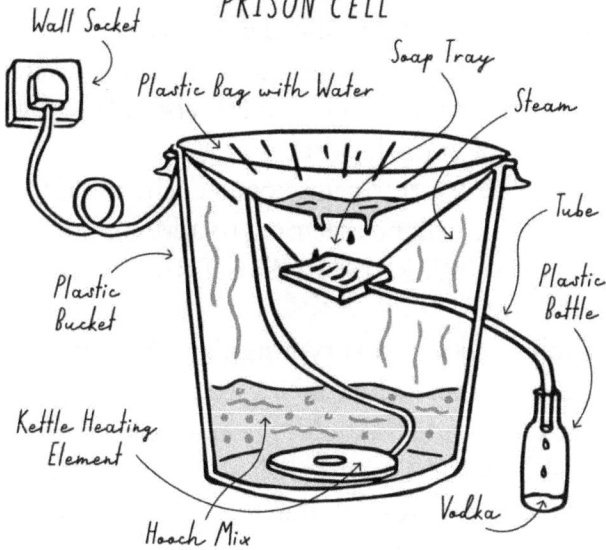

Vlad was up almost every night preparing his product.

In a sense he was therefore quite productive and hard working. He made his product and sold it. There was a lot of risk involved and he was making a lot of money.

He often tried to get me involved, saying I should making myself busy, rather than continue to waste my time reading books. According to his own world view, he was making the best of the situation.

The weeks with Vlad were by far the hardest I've had so far. It was incredibly stressful.

I did not have a moment for myself, the constant harassment was grating away at my mental reservoirs, I had no energy left.

Sometimes he would throw up all night. The whole cell would smell, there would be puke everywhere, and he wouldn't even remember.

I often toyed with the idea of ringing the bell and explaining everything to an officer, asking to be moved or asking for Vlad to be moved.

But I was too much of a chicken shit to do it.

What if it backfired and I wouldn't be moved? It would further sour the atmosphere and make things even harder. As much as Vlad was a little child mentally, he still had a huge physical presence and he was unpredictable and mentally unstable. I would have been lying if I'd said that I wasn't at least a little bit afraid of him.

There were some moments when I almost couldn't bear it anymore and thought I had no choice but to go ahead and ring the bell. Then something would happen that would make things a bit more bearable for a few hours – such as him passing out for a while – and I'd be able to collect myself and gather energy for the next onslaught.

One Monday morning, utterly unexpected, the cell door opened and an officer shouted into the cell, not seeming to address anyone in particular:

"SCHRAMM! TRANSFER! TRAINING PRISON! GET YOUR STUFF READY! 5 MINUTES!"

Nice! What followed was a very long day of waiting. First inside the holding cell of the hellhole; then inside the prison transport sweatbox; then at the other end inside the holding cell of the Training Prison and at property processing of the Training Prison. Transport days are very long, very boring but also very stressful. Imagine you're evicted from home and don't know where you're being taken.

So here I was once again, again sitting inside the cubicle of a prison van, my head leaning against the window looking out at the world that was passing me by. What a strange feeling. I wondered what it would be like to walk those streets, to walk into a shop. What would it be like to walk into a shop? I was playing with the idea in my head, trying to imagine what it would feel like.

What was different this time was that I had company. Castan and Lenny, two little children trapped inside the bodies of men.

"Are we there yet?"

"Hey, Officer: Do you have a sandwich at the front and something to drink? Can you slide some crisps under the door?"

"Hey Caspar, do you have any crisps?

"Hey Caspar..."

"Hey Officer..."

It was like driving with two children on the backseat.

Castan had more than a hundred convictions under his belt. *And I had thought Brendan's 42 were many.* He was a drug runner. I asked him if he had ever considered doing anything else, so he didn't have to come back to prison. "No" was his short answer. I left it at that.

Before we move on to the Training Prison, here a brief summary of my time inside the hellhole:

44

I had 5 different cellmates in less than 2 months.

3 of those smoked Spice. 4 out of 5 had an alcohol/drug problem outside, or at least problematic use.

5 out of 5 clearly had a mental health issue that hadn't been addressed properly and that certainly was not going to be addressed in prison.

If I include myself, that makes 5 out of 6 for substance abuse issues and at least 6 out of 6 for unresolved mental health issues.

I didn't understand this constant moving around and shifting of prisoners from cell to cell. It seemed to inefficient and so much unnecessary extra work.

Even more importantly, why don't prisoners get sent to the appropriate prison straight from court? Why does absolutely everyone have to go to the local hellhole first and then be transported to the appropriate prison? It seemed inefficient and unnecessary.

In retrospect, the reason I survived the hellhole was the curiosity of what prison was going to be like. It was an adventure. I was able to see a hidden world.

What grinds at you more than anything is the complete lack of purpose in prison.

There's no interest whatsoever in what prisoners are doing behind their cell doors.

Are they trying to change their ways and grow, rehabilitate themselves? Are they trying to educate themselves and read?

Or are they just watching TV all day and smoking Spice? The truth is that it doesn't make a difference to anyone. Nobody cares, it does not matter one bit.

The prison is struggling just to keep the most basic regime going: Getting people to lunch, to have a shower, canteen on Fridays, fresh air once or twice a week for a few minutes, medicines. It is nothing more than a human warehouse.

To expect more is pure fantasy as there simply aren't the resources. In any case, there's such chaos, such a churn of people coming and going, that it doesn't matter anyway.

For sentenced prisoners, who get moved on quickly, this is less of a problem. If you are a remand prisoner, however, you might end up spending your entire sentence in the hellhole, without any kind of rehabilitation taking place.

CHAPTER 2: THE TRAINING PRISON

ENTERING A NEW REALM

In my diary I wrote about the arrival at the Training Prison:

'The grass outside is covered in snow. I can smell freedom, even though I'm going to another prison.'

Remembering the contrast between the two prisons makes one realise that captivity isn't just captivity. There are such vast differences depending on which type of prison you're in.

The Training Prison immediately felt like freedom in comparison to the hellhole. My first few days and weeks there felt festive and dreamlike. My mood was almost euphoric.

In fact, I was so elated during the first days and weeks that the officers often had a laugh when they saw me: "Look, here comes the happiest prisoner in the UK!"

"Yaay, I'm in prison! Hooray!" "This guy is crazy..."

What created this effect? It was, firstly, the comparative quiet. And there was so much more space. Small wings surrounded by actual grass. We were in the countryside now, not in the middle of London.

Secondly, I now had a single cell for the first time. That was a huge difference, enormous. The single cell and the space meant I was able to breathe for the first time in a while.

What I also realised was how much the architecture of a prison will affect you psychologically. The difference in building design allowed the Training Prison to run a reasonably humane regime despite being in Covid-19 lockdown. Much smaller buildings housing fewer prisoners, and more surrounding green space, made it possible to isolate populations without having to lock everyone in for nearly 24 hours a day. Fresh air exercise could be given twice a day rather than twice a week. I now had at least 2 hours out of my cell every day. It's hard to convey how much of a difference those 2 hours made. In addition, being inside my cell suddenly wasn't stressful any more. I could just lie on my bed and enjoy the quiet. I could listen to the radio, or watch the TV channel I wanted. I could meditate. In the hellhole, I was on constant fight-and-flight mode; here I was able to wind down for the first time and feel a bit better. This opened the space in my head to really start thinking about what to do with my time in prison.

A BRIEF SETBACK

As always in prison when things were relatively good, the situation changed quickly. When I found out that I was to be moved into a double-cell after my induction period I was utterly devastated.

I had violated one of the main psychological rules of imprisonment: Don't ever get your hopes up. Always expect nothing and plenty of it. That way of thinking will make you more resilient and mentally strong, as it will be less easy to be disappointed, and if good things actually do happen, it will be an unexpected, fortunate bonus.

And already, there was a silver lining. My double cell in Unit 5 had a separate toilet with an actual door. Meaning you'd keep your human dignity when doing your business.

My new cellmate turned out to be a complete Spice head.

He was smoking all day from morning to night. He would pass out, sleep for a few hours, then get up and immediately smoke again. Then pass out again. That's how it went all day, every day. I was shocked to find out he spent £50 per day on Spice. He had sold his car on the outside and had already smoked through more than 4 grand.

It was painful to watch him. His canteen would immediately be gone every week as soon as he had it, to pay for various debts. On one occasion some of my canteen items actually went missing, and I was certain it was him (Who else would it have been?).

I asked him, but when he lied about it, I let it go, as there was no point in making a scene out of it; it wouldn't lead anywhere. Plus, it was only two cans of sardines...

Most shocking to me was to find out what Spice was actually made of in some cases.

Originally, it had been a synthetic cannabinoid that was sold legally in head shops until the Psychoactive Substance Act of 2016. After that it was still sold and used, but illegally.

Much of what was peddles inside prison as Spice, however, had little to do with the original product. Instead, it was often things like break fluids, rat poison, cleaning products, bleach. Whatever dissolvent, you name it.

An A4 sheet of paper gets drenched in chemicals at the cost of a few pennies, but gets sold in prison for hundreds of pounds. People get in trouble relating to debt. Ambulances have to be called to prison. Spiceheads turn into zombies, freak out, have psychotic episodes or seizures, get into fights, hurt themselves. I've seen several ambulances having to be sent to the Training prison because of Spice. When I recently read an article in which the ambulance service had complained about having to send an extraordinary number of ambulances to prison, it was clear to me that this was mostly because of Spice.[1]

On one occasion, my cellmate ran out of the stuff in the evening. He spent the whole night turning the cell upside down, looking for his shred of paper. Eventually, he gave up. The next morning, I could literally see the colour coming back into his face (you could always spot a Spicey by how sick they looked. Literally like someone who'd been poisoned) and he started talking to me in coherent sentences for the first time. It lasted until after lunch...

I witnessed another one of those moments of vulnerability that made you feel sorry for the situation that prisoners found themselves in. His grandma on the outside was dying and he spoke to her on the phone, sobbing.

INFO: HOW TO SOLVE THE SPICE PROBLEM IN PRISON

I will not go into the question of how much of a problem Spice is in prisons. It is an enormous problem. Mostly because compared to other drugs it is so easy to hide and to smuggle into prison. All you need is a sheet of paper.

As always with prohibition, any attempts at increased enforcements and crackdowns invariably always fail. You whack one mole and another comes up. The supply of drugs is always there, regardless of how much you police things and punish the people who get caught.

During my time at the Training Prison, one measure that was introduced was the photocopying of the sheets of paper that were sent in.

As a result, letters were piling up in the mailroom, as there weren't enough staff to photocopy at the same rate as letters arrived. Prisoners now had to wait weeks and sometimes months for letters. Hand-drawn artwork made by prisoner's children now arrived in grainy photocopied black-and-white.

And it did nothing to address the issue. One of the biggest outbreaks of Spice use was a few weeks after the new measure was introduced.

And the Spice problem is one that, at least in part, the prison service inflicted on itself when they started to crackdown on Cannabis use and introduce MDTs (Mandatory Drug test).

It first led to an increase in the use of Heroin and then later of Spice, because both drugs don't show in urine as long after consumption as cannabis does. Spice doesn't show at all, heroin only for a few days.

In short: The introduction of MDTs lead to prisoners abandoning the use of a relatively harmless substance (cannabis), in order to use two vastly more dangerous and harmful substances.[2]

The solution to the Spice problem in prison in my opinion is two-fold: The immediate and the long-term solution.

As an immediate solution, one has to look at why prisoners take Spice. If you are locked behind your door for nearly 24 hours a day for months and you have absolutely no purpose or anything meaningful to do, you are more likely to take Spice. The toll that an overcrowded, understaffed system takes on the mental health of prisoners directly translates into more Spice use. In addition, chaotic, overcrowded conditions without a proper regime make it more difficult to control drug use.

A functioning prison system with a solid regime in which prisoners have a purpose, are occupied and have meaningful things to do will, without question, lead to at least some decrease in use.

The long-term solution that I propose is more controversial.

Once cannabis is legalised in the UK – which it will be at some point – the prison service should offer it on the canteen. Use of cannabis could be controlled and monitored. Compared to Spice, it would be less expensive, and fewer prisoners would get into debt with others, having to constantly move wings and leading to all sorts of behavioural problems. Fewer ambulances would have to be called as cannabis is relatively harmless compared to Spice. There is no question that given the choice, many prisoners would smoke the occasional spliff to feel better and more relaxed, rather than getting into all the trouble that Spice brings with it. Not everyone, but many.

Many reading this will think I'm completely out of my mind to suggest giving cannabis to prisoners: *"What next? A Bob Marley tribute act? Porridge and red wine? Maybe we should ask Tim Martin of Wetherspoon's to run prisons?"*

My experience in prison tells me that more prisoners are taking drugs than anyone wants to admit and that enforcement simply doesn't work.

If you think my cannabis idea is flawed, then you'll have to admit that the only alternative is creating better prisons with a functioning, purposeful regime.

SETTLING DOWN FOR A YEAR (WHEN NOTHING HAPPENED)

Cell 77 in unit 25 of the Training Prison, west site, would become my permanent home for the next year.

Of course, I didn't know that at the time: you never knew what happened next in prison, or how long you were going to stay in one place.

Each unit in the Training Prison was a fenced-off compound that included the building and the yard.

Unit 25 was designed like a horseshoe or a U; two wings on each side; with offices and the servery in the middle. The wings comprised two floors of normal ceiling height with cells on both sides. It was like a hospital or army barracks in character. The building was surrounded by the yard which included an access road, lots of grass, benches and a few outdoor exercise machines.

The large yard meant I could actually go for a run during the exercise periods!

UNIT 25 TRAINING PRISON

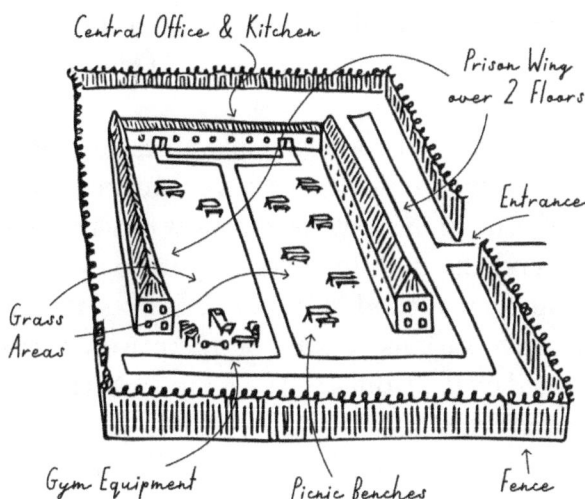

Central Office & Kitchen

Prison Wing over 2 Floors

Entrance

Grass Areas

Gym Equipment

Picnic Benches

Fence

The whole compound housed 80 prisoners and occupied about the same ground area as a 3-floor Victorian prison wing for 400 prisoners. You can imagine the difference in overall atmosphere the reduced prisoner-density made.

The building was comparatively modern (mid-20th century) and the cells were singles with an en-suite shower and toilet.

Sounds like a hotel, doesn't it? It was still prison. You still couldn't nip down to the shops.

There was also less of a coming-and-going of prisoners. Many prisoners had been staying at the unit for many months or even longer than a year.

Even though the prison still ran a Covid regime, there was at least a 1hr fresh-air exercise period twice a day, plus social and domestics periods where you could mingle with other prisoners inside the building.

All of this completely changed the character of what incarceration was like for me. I was able to settle into an actual routine for the first time.

As some prisoners had been staying at the unit for a while, there was a sense of community that I hadn't experienced before. You were able to get to know people a little bit better during the afternoon walks in the yard and the talks on the corridor or in someone's cell.

It was also where I met Bill, the only real friend I made in prison.

When I first saw him sitting on the bench in the yard, I thought he looked like a shorter and slightly chubbier version of Florian Henckel von Donnersmarck, the German film director.

For some reason something about him shouted theatre or film. Maybe it was just the book on the structure of plays ('How to read a play') that he was reading.

He also occupied the cell opposite of mine, so over time, we just naturally started talking. It was clear that we were both complete outliers in terms of level of education compared to most other inmates.

Whereas I'd spend the morning exercise session going for a run, the afternoon we'd usually walk and talk about our lives and politics.

Whilst many conversations centred on the prison system, not all did. We were often joined by Paul, Bill's cell neighbour. At times, conversations became more heated when topics such as Brexit were approached. Level of education mostly predicted one's opinion on Brexit, just as it did in the outside world.

Two other guys you could have a good conversation with were Pat & Barry, both from Ireland. Pat was a long-term prisoner who had already served 18 years and had still many years to go. It was never clear what the offence was, but it must have been something severe. He was always wearing long-sleeved clothes, which indicated to me that he must have self-harmed at some point. Or was even self-harming, still.

He was a very nice guy, but at the same time, you would notice that he lacked self-control. He was constantly interrupting you and not letting you finish your sentences, which became annoying after a while. If you tried pointing it out to him, he would interrupt you as you did so. He seemed smart and knowledgeable, and in no way ever did he seem like a dangerous individual to me. At the same time, however, there was also clearly something 'off' about him. Something wasn't quite right, but it was difficult to pin down what it was.

Barry was probably – together with Bill – the most 'normal' prisoner I met (whatever that means). He had a large amount of books in his cell. We occasionally exchanged books and did have some really good conversations.

From what I understood he was an accountant and there had been a large court case, which he obviously lost in the end. Despite being low risk, he wasn't yet allowed in open conditions, due to some outstanding financial issues. If you had a 'confiscation order', meaning you owed money to the government, you weren't allowed in open conditions. This is what happened in the case of many drug dealers. They have to return the money they earned through criminal activity to the government. Very often, of course, that money doesn't exist anymore because it is already spent.

One thing I noticed during that time is that you stop wondering what people are in for. When you arrive in prison, that's always the burning question: '*I wonder what he's in for...*'

After a while, the question loses its meaning. You stop caring and realise that, mostly, it doesn't make a difference. Once you start becoming part of the prisoner community, you dislike how society stereotypes criminals and feel disgusted by the idea of putting a label on someone, judging them solely by what they've done, often years ago. Between 16 and 26 is the age when most crimes are committed, with the rate steadily dropping as one gets older.[4] Someone at 40 who has committed a crime 20 years ago simply isn't the same person anymore. I used to feel very differently about this, thinking people wouldn't change.

However, when prisoners talked about their crimes or some fight they had with someone, I usually switched off or walked away. It just didn't interest me. I wasn't the least interested in gossip or the private lives of other prisoners.

What I was interested in was the politics – how the prison system was run and the implications of that for society.

And that's why it was so great during that time to have a few people that I could have meaningful conversations with.

Routine

The week was broken down into 'highlights' that you could look forward to. By far the biggest highlight was Wednesday, when the library box arrived.

The library was at that moment still closed due to Covid, but what you could do was order books via a form. They arrived each Wednesday, a very big day.

As you didn't know which books were actually available in the library, you had to fill in order forms 'blindly', i.e. guessing which titles they might have.

Fortunately, however, as the library was able to order in books in from other county libraries, you would often get what you wanted, albeit with a long delay of often weeks.

As you never knew which books would arrive, the library box was a surprise to look forward to each week.

And a horrible surprise if there weren't any books in it. It meant you had to wait another whole week. An empty library box was so dispiriting, it could plunge me into a deep depression.

What's interesting to note here is how small things in prison can really affect you. Your world becomes very small, with minor things such as an empty library box becoming a catastrophe.

Other 'highlights' were canteen day, gym day or even just the day the canteen sheets or menu sheets could be filled out.

A very important daily highlight was the newspaper.

Without internet, this was my connection to the outside world. It allowed me to remember that I was still there and provided a way to still make me feel part of society. I could stay informed on what was going on. A special interest was anything that was written about prisons. I'd read an article and then discuss it with other inmates.

Even if I didn't have access to Netflix or Disney+, at least I could find out about new shows and films, read reviews and make a mental note of what to watch after my release. The book review section was vital as it provided me with titles that I could try to order from the library.

Nearly equally important was the radio. It's the connection to the outside world that made it so meaningful to me. And the company that it gave me in my cell. Radio makes you feel like you're not alone, much more so than the TV.

It's also important not to underestimate the power of music during dark times. Music can be a soul-saviour.

Jeremy Vine on BBC2 would coincide with the time we were locked in after lunch; I'd therefore listen to it almost every day. Topics covered could then be discussed during the afternoon walk.

'Sounds of the 80s' with Gary Davies was a big one for me every Saturday evening at 8. I've always loved 80s music and I really liked Gary's presenting style. Just warm, kind and pleasant.

Every weekday evening there was Clara Amfo and Jack Saunders on BBC1. I would usually read and have the radio in the background.

If there was something good, I'd watch a film or a documentary on BBC. Also things like 'BBC Panorama' and 'Question Time'.

All the other channels I mostly avoided, especially for films, as I couldn't stand the commercials every 10 minutes. Film 4 was one of the worst culprits in that regard. The exception was occasionally 'The Chase' as it was on just after we collected our dinner.

I also continued devouring every bit of literature or TV program that had to do with prison. I read the 'Inside Times' (the prison newspaper sent to prisons) every month and even contributed to it. Trying to inform myself was my way of dealing with the situation. What therefore interested me not so much were sensational prison diaries that glorified crime, but those that went into the psychological aspects of imprisonment and criticised the system. Other prisoners had a different approach. When I mentioned a prison program to watch on TV, Paul's reply (perhaps understandably) was: "I'm already living this shit. Don't need to see it on TV also."

Access to materials and information was my single biggest frustration. Imagine how difficult it is to find out anything if you don't have the internet and can't go anywhere. It's a nightmare.

Often, the bibliography of a book from the library would open the road for further names of titles that I could try to order. Most often, however, you had to call people on the phone for information.

"Can you please look this up for me, Bill?" "Is there a book called...?" "Does it say anything about..." I hated being so reliant on other people, it really made you feel like a disabled person needing help for everything. And it took forever to get a simple answer that would take two seconds on google.

When we had long discussions on the wing, sometimes about silly subjects such as whether the actor Peter Capaldi and the singer Lewis Capaldi were related (a conversation that lasted a good twenty minutes), it was often necessary to call someone on the outside for clarification. (I called Bill, who found out they were second cousins.)

Catalogue Orders

In theory, it was possible to order books on Amazon. Catalogue orders could also be made for clothes, DVD players and other appliances on Argos, and DVDs, CDs and games on GEMA (a catalogue specifically for prisons).

In practice, however, it was a process that took so long you might as well have left it. 4-5 months from order to arrival was not unusual. (For something that if ordered today would arrive at prison reception tomorrow.)

When I arrived at the Training Prison, I ordered a DVD player on Argos. That took about 3 months. For some books ordered later on Amazon, it took even longer.

Often, you placed an order, and 6 weeks later you would receive a notification saying the item was out of stock. So you had to start the whole process again from scratch.

As nothing was digital, you couldn't even look into the status of your order. There was no indication when it might arrive. It might be 4 weeks, it might also be 16.

You could also get a birthday parcel sent in.

The one that my mom sent me I received about 9 months after she had sent it. (When I had already been at the next prison for 3 months.) Apart from books it contained some family photos of sentimental value.

Why did all of this take so long? The answer lies with what happened when ordered parcels arrived at the prison.

INFO: PARCELS AND PROPERTY – A COMPLETE DISASTER

All parcels that came in to the prison had to be security checked before they could be passed on to the prisoner for obvious reasons. Due to an enormous backlog of parcels that were already piling up at reception, waiting to be security-checked and processed, it could take many months until a parcel that had arrived at the prison was actually in possession of the prisoner to whom it was for.

That prisoner might have in the meantime moved prison, so it had to be sent to another prison. That was a regular occurrence. Whenever you moved prison, you were still missing property from your old prison and it would take months and months to get it. Often it was lost altogether.

Why the chaos? Quite simply lack of resources and staff. For a prison of 1300 prisoners at the Training Prison there was really only one officer who dealt with property reception. And if there was a shortage of staff he'd be the first to be pulled to fill in for other jobs.

A further aggravating factor was that the reception of the west site had been closed and combined with the main site reception to save costs.

To his absolute credit, the governor of the prison often had discussion forums with representatives of prisoners from each wing of the prison. Each time the discussions were the same. Frustrations about property reception. People waiting months and months for their property.

The governor tried to blame it on people sending in items that aren't allowed and thereby clogging up everything. That might be a small factor, but wasn't the main issue. The main issue was that reception was catastrophically understaffed.

A prison officer who worked at the prison had confided to me that it had been like that for more than 20 years.

In fact, I read a prison inspection report from the year 2018 which stated: "Unfortunately, the problems with processing of prisoners' property still haven't been resolved."

The governor was clearly frustrated, and to me it was also clear that he couldn't do anything about it. He wasn't allocated or allowed the resources to change the situation.

What annoyed me also was that there was no difference made between items in terms of whether they are rehabilitative or pure leisure. In my view, items that are educational, such as books or language courses should have been prioritised over clothes and video games, but that wasn't the case.

Apart from exchanging handwritten letters with friends, I also continued writing in my diary. Less frequent, as I didn't need it as much to cope as I did at the hellhole. There it had been my tool to deal with the daily frustration and pain.

Re-reading that diary now, it's mostly useless, embarrassing rubbish. Being at peace with the world ('*I can hear the birds chirping in the morning when I do my meditation*'), profound wisdom ('*Whether I sleep in this prison bed, my bed in Wembley or my bed back home in Germany, in the grand scheme of things it doesn't make a difference...*'), wishes for the future ('*If I had one wish in the world, it would be never having to share a cell again.*') and the usual rantings about how bad and inadequate the prison system is. It's especially the catalogue order and long delays in ordering books that during this time seemed to have been the greatest sources of frustration and anger.

I had also joined a prison writing program, run by the Arkbound Foundation. It involved a mentorship program. My mentor would read my handwritten short stories that I sent to him via mail and give ideas for improvement.

I also took part in a writing competition for Koestler Arts. The Koestler awards are a huge yearly completion that all prisoners can take part in. Art forms include crafts, drawing, painting and many forms of writing. Over 3500 prisoners take part every year and Koestler holds a yearly exhibition in the South Bank, displaying the best artworks. For my short story 'Free as a jail-pigeon' I received a £25 prize.

Education

I abandoned original plans to finish my psychology degree as I couldn't get all my passed modules accredited. I had been in year 3, passed my dissertation and was only missing some modules. With the Open University here in prison, I would have needed to start almost from the beginning and pay the full £9000 student fee per year, which simply wasn't worth it.

Instead, I applied for an Italian language course funded by the Prison Education Trust. The PET is a charity that funds a variety of courses for prisoners. You applied through the education department of the prison.

My application was successful and I received my course materials – audio CDs and books – within 2 months. As it went via education and the course was sent straight to education, I was able to bypass the usual problems with parcels at reception.

I was now able to learn Italian in my cell with a full course that took me from beginner to advanced learner. What I had been doing before is to borrow foreign language books in the library and read them with the help of my dictionaries. Every time I didn't know a word, I wrote it down to learn it. It was slow at the beginning and I often wasn't able to identify whether words were verbs or nouns, as I didn't know all the different verb conjugations. But you can guess quite a lot if you know most words in a sentence and through the context of the storyline. And over time, it gets easier and easier.

That was the best option for me, as most of the courses the education department of the prison had on offer were English and Maths for inmates who hadn't finished high school. There were also vocational courses such as bricklaying, plumbing and electrics.

Missing were art or creative courses. I've heard through the grapevine that the education governor didn't believe in them.

There was one exception, however. The Synergy theatre group offered a scriptwriting course. Synergy was set up in 2000 by Esther Baker. Its aim is to use drama to help and educate people at risk, such as prisoners. It shows plays in the community, often staged by ex-prisoners, and runs courses across prisons in the UK.

This would have been right up my street. Unfortunately, there were only 5 places and a long waiting list. I applied, but didn't get in as others came before me.

INFO: EDUCATION

Around 50% of inmates have literacy and numeracy competency levels below the average 11-year-old.[3]
This shows how much of a factor education is in offending and how much potential there is to reduce reoffending by providing education in prison.

More than that, education offers prisoners a perspective, a different way of seeing and understanding the world. Many prisoners have self-esteem issues and mental health problems that could equally addressed by empowering them through education.

Unfortunately, the education currently provided in prison is simply inadequate and insufficient. There are some fantastic people working in prison education who do their best and teach their classes with passion, but the problem is structural.

Education in prison is a side show, rather than the main event it should be. The problem is the structure of the prison regime, with its high emphasis on security, which does not allow for education to take centre stage.

Just the very basics of the regime (lunch, dinner, medication, exercise, social) require an enormous amount of time and resources. At the Training prison, my cell door was unlocked and locked again at least 6 or 7 times a day. You get let out at 8, locked back in at 11; let out at 11.30 for lunch, locked back in straight after; let out at 2, locked back in at 4; let out at 4.30 for dinner, then locked back straight after.

The education building is in a different part of the prison than the residential wings, which means officers need to escort you. If there is a lack of staff, you won't be able to go to education.

This means that at best, prisoners can expect are a few hours of education each week. That is simply not enough for people who have left school when they were 11 and have to catch up on absolutely everything.

What should be possible is for prisoners to spend the day inside the education building and have lunch there.

In terms of what is taught in educations are level 1 and level 2 English and Maths, which are so basic, they take you to the level of an 7th or 8th grader. Really, they are most suitable for foreigners that are starting to learn English. And those are mostly the only two subjects that are taught.

At the minimum, it should be possible for inmates to re-do their GCSE's.

To me, the state of prison education is a prime example of why the entire system is failing.

Education should be seen as one of the most important things that happen in prison, not as a side show.

If you think that I live in fantasy land if I truly believe that every single prisoner is keen on improving his education, you are right. And, of course, many have learning difficulties.

But these issues can be addressed. Many prisoners are resistant to education because they have only had bad experiences in school. With a little support and nurturing, this can be addressed in many cases.

In addition, I am in favour of incentives for education. If education were tied to sentence length, meaning prisoners could reduce their sentence length by engaging in education, there would be a lot less resistance.

The worst we can do is to accept the idea that most prisoners are 'lost causes' and therefore not worth taking a chance for. This attitude is costing society dear.

Mental Health

I now also had the opportunity to meet with a therapist. Daisy worked for the Forward Trust, another charity. I found the sessions really helpful. What was great was to be able to talk to someone about the things that went on in my head. The more intimate things you wouldn't necessarily share with the other inmates. Conversations, especially conversations with trained professionals that are in a position to help you, were so important but missing.

Unfortunately, we only had a few sessions. I would have loved to continue and have regular, long-term psychotherapy. This had to wait until after my release. Daisy was one of only two psychologists working at the prison; and there were many prisoners that had more acute mental problems than I had.

As our sessions came to an end, Daisy recommended me to work as a peer mentor for the Forward Trust, as she noted how interested I was in mental health.

There was an interview process with Hillary, the coordinator, and I got the job. The pay was £18 per week. And it gave me the privilege of moving freely between the units of the prison (at certain times).

Peer Mentoring

This was my first paid prison job! It was great to be able to move around the prison and speak to prisoners in other units. The idea was that we would present ourselves in other units, wearing our 'Forward Trust' t-shirts, having our presence announced on the tannoy, and people that needed help would approach us. It didn't quite work out like that.

We thought the problem was that people weren't necessarily open to come forward so openly and make themselves vulnerable. We therefore put flyers underneath people's cell doors, but that didn't work much better, either. At no point did I have more than one or two mentees.

To be honest, the whole thing never really took off. It was all quite lacklustre and there wasn't enough supervision and planning to really get it going. We mostly just hung around the units and had a chat.

Overall, I still think the mentorship thing to be a great idea, maybe with a better implementation. What worried me was that programs like this gave the illusion that help was available in prison, when it clearly wasn't. (Or at least not enough of it.)

As a mentor, I could have confidential conversations with other prisoners. They would confide in me. And, of course, as someone with the same shared experience I could give some advice. Some prisoners might prefer to speak to a fellow prisoner; you are on the same wavelength. But I wasn't a mental health professional, and even my training as mentor was minimal.

What were needed were more trained therapists, with peer mentors being there as support, under supervision. But peer mentors as a substitute for sufficient professional help just didn't seem right.

I need to mention one of my mentees, Nigel, although I'd rather forget about him. In my capacity as mentor, I did get to know him better than most other prisoners and was hearing some quite private and intimate details of his life. Due to confidentiality, I cannot reveal any of the things he told me, nor do I want to.

I want to mention him because he was a domestic abuser.

Some of the things that he told me were disconcerting and his perspective was clearly warped. I had never heard of anyone forcing his partner to subject themselves to a lie detector test before, and it's a mystery to me why anyone would want to stay with a person like that. But of course, it's not that easy. The matter is complex and there are reasons why abused women stay with their partners.

He was convinced that his sentence was unjust, exaggerated and that he had hardly done anything. It was his partner who had been twisting the facts. I didn't believe a word of what he was saying.

Whenever you saw him, the alarm bells went off.

It was a gut feeling that made you want to take a wide berth. There was something about him that was profoundly weird, even a bit twisted. Already the shape of his head struck me as abnormal – so squared and edgy, like Herman Munster.

Then at other times, he was cracking a joke and seemed normal, even charming.

I was struggling with the fact that he had four children. Nigel is an example of someone where I would say, yes, he absolutely needs to be in prison, or in some other secure facility. But he also clearly needs intense mental health support to challenge his warped perception of things and get to the bottom of his disorders.

Then there was DeVito. He was one of the people that I had most contact with at the Training prison. We didn't become friends in the same way as with Bill, but we did have some laughs. He was a genuinely good guy, with his offence not being in line with what you saw in front of you. He moved into the cell opposite of mine, after Bill was released.

Bill had done his 5 months (which went so quick) and was on his way home to be put on a home detention curfew for another few months. Meaning he received an ankle tag and was not allowed to leave the house from 1900hrs to 0700hrs.

I did stay in contact with Bill and we would often talk on the phone. He became one of my main links to the outside world and I would call him often to ask questions or look something up. What a friend, spending hours on the phone every week listening to my gripes and grievances about prison life.

But back to DeVito. The reason he had this nickname was that, as you might guess, he looked like Danny DeVito. Vaguely, very vaguely. Maybe. I didn't see it to be honest, maybe a little. Something in the face was similar, but he was a lot slimmer and not quite as short.

As he was in the cell opposite, we became quite close.

He was 18 years into his life sentence for murder and was up for parole, as his tariff had been 15 years. A tariff is the minimum term someone with a life sentence has to serve. Once the tariff is reached, the offender will sit in front of the parole board every two years, which decides whether he can be safely released back into society.

What happened was that he beat a suspected paedophile to death with a guitar. Actually, he began beating him with his hands, then saw the guitar leaning against the wall in the room and finished off the job with that.

The intention hadn't been to kill, it was a heat-of-the-moment situation fuelled by crack cocaine and anger.

The paedo aspect was a major mitigating factor in DeVitos opinion. He even said to me once that he should have received a medal rather than a murder conviction. I saw it differently.

What it highlighted was the extreme attitude amongst prisoners towards sex-offenders – also known as nonces – I often encountered.

INFO: NONCES – A NON-HUMAN SUB-SPECIES OF PRISONER (ACCORDING TO SOME...)

In the eyes of many a prisoner, sex-offenders were in a completely different category from everyone else in prison. They were sub-human scum. Compared to sex-offenders, all other prisoners were nobility.

They were hated, despised, and usually had to be kept in separate units or even solitary confinement for their own protection. If they were amongst the general prison population, they had to keep their offence secret as to not get brutally attacked sooner or later. What explained this attitude of prisoners toward their own?

In my view, it was quite simple. You always need someone who's worse than you, in order to be able to feel better about yourself. If you're a convicted murderer that's pretty difficult – the bar is low. But at least you can always convince yourself that you're not a sex offender. They're the real scum.

What is hypocritical about the attitude towards sex offenders in prison is that prisoners expect the public to let go of prejudice and not judge all of them alike. Yet prisoners demonstrate exactly the same prejudice when it comes to nonces.

The fact is that sex offender is a huge category with a large variety of different offences. You do not know that someone is a paedophile if he is a convicted sex offender. You also never know the details of the conviction as you weren't there.

It has to be said, however, that DeVito was one of the nicest people I met in prison, despite his offence that made you take a step back. He was always good for a laugh.

Whilst I thought that he should be released as he'd done his time and paid for his mistake, it was also clear that he hadn't worked through his issues as much as you would expect after 18 years.

He still had a problem with substances and there seemed to be some issues that were unresolved. I also wondered if something had happened in his childhood that led him to have this extreme reaction towards sex offenders. There was an inner anger somewhere that was suppressed.

I also often noticed that he didn't know what to do with himself, which I thought was odd for someone of his age.

All complete speculation, but those are the questions you are asking yourself.

Nevertheless, he had done is time and if he didn't get all the support he might have needed, it wasn't entirely his fault. He has paid the price for his actions in full and now he should have been allowed out. 18 years was enough – what was the point of keeping him longer? You would gain absolutely nothing.

I did not see evil in DeVito. What I saw was an inner anger, trauma, unresolved issues, hurt and pain; but not evil.

Was he still a danger? Who can say for sure.

The weeks and months had been flying by. It was the solid routine, the purpose I managed to give myself (although frustrated at times), the good social contacts, plus the occupation as peer mentor that made me a happy prisoner during that period.

Despite the fact that I managed to give myself a purpose and a structure, there was always this overall feeling of senselessness and lack of purpose that pervaded prison life. It was all a bit pointless, the days just drifting by.

This often made me think of the prison officers. Surely, they must have been thinking: What am I actually doing here?

What was missing was a clear mission of what prison was supposed to do (Other than just to lock people up). Sure, there was some education and other things, but nothing was done with conviction, nothing ultimately mattered. This led me to formulate the ultimate two prison rules.

THE ULTIMATE 2 PRISON RULES:

1. Nobody should escape

2. Nobody should get hurt (Officer or Prisoner)

Apart from 1 and 2, nothing matters and nobody gives a fuck about anything.

That's an exaggeration, of course. But it was often the general feeling.

The other theory that I couldn't shake off, as stupid as it was, was that prisoners were on average shorter than the general population.

I came up with this idea when we had to wait for access to the gym.

As it was raining, we were all lined up in a long row with our backs against the building to seek shelter from the rain under the little roof. As I was looking down this long row of at least 30 prisoners, I realised I was by far the tallest of all of them, except one or two.

As ridiculous as the idea that prisoners are shorter than average might sound, there's actually some evidence to support it.

INFO: ARE PRISONERS SHORTER THAN AVERAGE?

The research paper "Short criminals: stature and crime in early America." (2010) by Howard Bodenhorn et al. looked at the height of convicts in Philadelphia between 1826 and 1876, and found exactly that.

In the case of black convicts, height was compared to black slaves. For white convicts, the comparison was made with Army enlistants. In both cases, the convicts were on average significantly shorter than the non-prison population.[4]

Biological determinism has of course been discredited.

So the idea that there is a direct link or that being short makes you a criminal is nonsense.[5]

However, it is true that physical attributes such as attractiveness, obesity and height translate into different chances of success in the job market.[6]

It could therefore well be that short individuals are on average less likely to get a good job and therefore more likely to be driven towards criminality.

A Real Surprise

My relatively happy existence and the steady, productive routine I had found were brutally interrupted when an Immigration Officer came to see me.

He informed me that as a Foreign National with a sentence of more than 12 months I was liable for deportation.

This came as a complete shock and surprise – something I hadn't seen coming at all.

I had been living in the UK for over 15 years and didn't see myself as a foreigner – London was my home.

But under the Immigration Act of 1971, any offender who is not a UK citizen and has a sentence of over 12 months is automatically considered for deportation.[7]

The Immigration officer explained the situation to me.

I had two options:

I could get deported voluntarily. This would reduce my sentence by 12 months. It would mean that I would be on a flight to Germany in a little more than a year's time. But it would also mean that I'd be banned from the UK and couldn't come back. He showed me a piece of paper to sign, should this be my preference.

The other option was to fight my deportation and try to explain why deportation would be disproportionate and I should be allowed to stay in the country.

I would have to send a letter to the home office making my case. There was no guarantee my argument would be accepted and I could still get deported anyway.

In addition, if I chose the 2nd option and my request to be allowed to stay in the country would be unsuccessful I would lose the reduction of my sentence and would have to serve the full 3 years in prison before being deported. It was a huge gamble.

The first option meant certainty and just one more year in prison, rather than two. But, it would also mean deportation from the place that was home.

The second option meant utter uncertainty and serving my sentence in limbo, not knowing what would happen afterwards. It was not expected that the home office would make the decision before the end of my sentence; I would therefore have to spend the rest of my sentence with the uncertainty of not knowing whether I'll be able to stay in the UK.

"I want to stay in the country", I told the officer.

He took the deportation declaration with him and handed me the other sheet. "I thought so."

"Basically, what they know about you is the bad stuff. They know about the offence", he told me. "What they don't know is all the good you've done. Your work in the film industry, for example. Write and tell them about the good."

"What are my chances? How many people get deported and how many get to stay?"

He couldn't give me a concrete answer, but said:

"I think you have a strong case."

He seemed to like me and was impressed with my work in the film industry. He asked me a lot of questions about that, and we had a nice, friendly conversation. It seemed to me he thought that I wasn't a bad person, but just had made a mistake.

But he was not the one who would make the decision.

This really was something that I had not expected to happen, a real curveball.

I was cursing the fact that I never obtained dual citizenship.

There was a brief moment after Brexit when I thought I should better do so. But then the EU settlement scheme was introduced, guaranteeing all the rights and indefinite leave to remain to any EU citizen who'd been in the UK for over 10 years, so there simply wasn't the necessity.

I had two weeks to write the letter to the home office in Croydon, but I could submit supporting evidence later.

Over the next few days I spent the evenings drafting the letter. It was hard work as I had to write everything by hand.

I outlined my whole life story, from arrival in the UK in 2006 to today, mostly concentrating on my work experience. I named all the addresses that I had lived at, which meant I had to call Bill because I couldn't remember all of them. I outlined how I broke into the film industry, going to a screening at the Genesis Cinema in Whitechapel and asking Location Manager Michael Harm for his email address. I outlined how that gave me my first break and I started working as a runner, slowly working my way up over the years. I mentioned the projects I was most proud of.

The letter came to about 14 handwritten pages I think. I also added all the 6 references I used in court – all work references from friends and bosses. These were glowing references that spoke of my professionalism and integrity at work, all 6 of them. They didn't help me in court, but I knew for this they would help me.

I sent that off and then tried to gather the evidence I needed to state my case. One very lucky circumstance was that the payroll for nearly all film productions was done by one single company – Sargent Disc Ltd. I was able to send them a letter and obtain all payslips going back to 2011. This was crucial as it proved not just that I had been working constantly for over 10 years, but also that I had had a good income and had continually been paying tax for over 10 years.

The main argument that I put forward was that deportation would be disproportionate as I was a decent, hard-working and honest person who is a contributor to society in a positive manner, but has made one huge mistake that isn't reflective of his character. And who has to offer lots to society in the future.

My main 6 points were: 1. Resident in the UK for over 15 years, 2. Positive contribution through work in the film industry, 3. Full integration into British society, 4. Overall good character, 5. Genuine remorse and rehabilitation, 6. Future potential.

I added a table indicating which piece of evidence would support which point.

I also tried to make the passionate point that London was my home and that I cared a lot about Britain and was very engaged politically. I also cared about people and wanted to be a positive influence and a force for good, despite my offence. It wasn't difficult to write all of this, because it was true.

I was convinced that anyone reading what I had put together would conclude that it would be wrong to deport me. But that didn't mean anything. The political situation was that the more foreign criminals were deported, the better it looked in the eyes of the government. Maybe home office immigration caseworkers were under pressure to get their numbers as high as possible, and didn't always have a choice. There was a lot of uncertainty for me. It was a horrible situation to have this uncertainty hanging over me.

All of this also meant that as a foreign national, at some point I would be transferred to a foreign national prison.

It was an unpleasant thought, as I had found my routine on unit 25.

Things were fine and they could have happily gone on like this until my release. Or better, I would have been categorised D Cat and sent to an open prison like everyone else.

But going to a foreign national prison seemed like a nightmare. You just knew that it was going to be awful.

When just weeks later I was then asked whether I wanted to go to a foreign national prison up north, I declined. I know it was inevitable that I'd have to go eventually, but didn't want to accept it.

Until one day, I simply wasn't given the choice.

When you get transferred to another prison, you are not being told beforehand.

It might be a normal Wednesday morning, you prepare yourself for exercise, have your morning coffee. Then the door opens and you are being told to pack your stuff and be ready in 5 minutes to go.

It is very traumatic, like a forceful eviction.

You have also no idea where you are being sent to and what it will be like there. It is all very stressful and anxiety-inducing.

And of course, what followed was the usual endless waiting in holding cells. I met a guy named Tinto.

He was from Unit 23. "It's stressful, man, it's stressful." He kept saying. He told me how he had had a phone in his cell and was used to watching Netflix. He obviously had to leave it in the unit. I asked him how much phones cost in prison. I couldn't believe his answer. It could go into the thousands, but usually 800 or 900 quid.

CHAPTER 3: THE FOREIGN NATIONAL PRISON

SHIT AND MISERY

Whenever I just hear the name of the town in which the Foreign National Prison was located, it makes me feel slightly sick. I'll never be able to go to that town again in my life, out of sheer fear that someone might grab me off the street and force me to go back to that prison: "There's been a mistake. You need to go back."

If there is such a thing as hell, it's the Foreign National Prison.

Of course, it was a double-cell again. Of course it was. I thought I had this nightmare behind me and here I was. It would have simply been too good to be true to have been able to finish the rest of my sentence without the torture of having to share a cell.

Never violate the golden rule of always expecting the worst and lots of it! It will come to bite you....

The silver lining was that most of the cells in the prison were actually singles and I would be moved to a single cell after the induction period of 3-4 weeks. Mentally I was heavily clinging on to that silver lining. I was hanging onto it by a very thin thread.

Incredibly, this time we were even locked in our cells 24hrs a day for the first week of quarantine.

The full quarantine was a Covid protection measure. Once you had had two negative tests, you were out of quarantine.

The reason the lockdown was so extreme was once again architectural. The Foreign National is a very old prison, with the induction wing one of the oldest in the country (although renovated recently). One open wing over three floors meant cohorts couldn't be easily isolated. When you were in induction quarantine, the only time you could have your shower was when everyone else was locked up over lunch. There was no exercise, nothing. It really was essentially a 24-hour bang up behind your cell doors.

And, of course, the toilet was once again part of the living room furniture. There wasn't even a curtain. The toilet seat was right next to the lunch table, as the cell was so small.

The cell was so small; we couldn't even empty our bags because there wouldn't have been the space to put things. Our bags were all piled up in the corner behind the bed opposite the toilet. There was also no space for me to do my essential daily running on the spot.

When Tinto was sitting at the table, I was just about able to squeeze passed him and if he leaned forward as far as he could. It was so annoying.

Once again, it was clearly a single cell that had been forcefully mutilated to fit two people and a double bunk bed in.

Things became marginally better after the first week, once the quarantine was over and we had some fresh-air exercise.

In a yard that can only be described as a rat cage.

The wing housed 140 prisoners, but if there were more than 30 people in the yard it was full. There was a square patch of grass in the middle and tarmac around it. You ran around the square taking a left turn every 15 meters (or a right turn if you switched directions). If there were a handful of people going for a run at the same time it felt like the M25. That's what I called it, the M25. And our yard was actually the best yard of all the 4 wings of the prison.

I was lucky with my cellmate, although I failed to appreciate at the time. He was clean and didn't have any nasty habits.

Tinto originally hailed from Venezuela but was getting himself deported to Spain as he had Spanish family (he had signed the paper, now getting a reduction of 12 months off his sentence). That was despite the fact that he had children in the UK.

He had been given a fixed 10-year sentence for assault, so had to do 4 (minus the 1 due to getting deported). To me 10 years seemed very steep for a beating up, but you never knew, maybe there was more to it.

RUNNING AROUND THE M25 IN THE RATCAGE

One thing you learn is to never trust subjective accounts of prisoners.

He seemed honest to me, however. We did get along. He said he appreciated the fact that I had no interest in talking about 'street stuff'. Everybody was always just talking 'street'. I understood what he meant, even though I didn't.

However he was, it didn't change the fact that he was massively going on my nerves.

That wasn't his fault, it's simply what happens when you force two people into a space that is hardly large enough for one person, and then lock them up 24hrs.

As soon as Tinto woke up, he took a dump. Imagine sitting at the desk reading and writing, maybe drinking your coffee and the person next to you takes a shit.

Then he'd have his morning drink in a plastic cup, loudly slurping it. A thousand tiny, tiny slurps. Morning after morning. Soon enough, every one of them became as painful as a dagger being rammed into my chest. A thousand small daggers, killing me slowly day after day, like piranhas eating away at your flesh, bite by bite.

Then there were the meal times. Again, he wasn't specifically loud or impolite; it's just that I can't stand having to listen to someone else eat food in such close proximity. It's not like sitting around the dinner table at home. Because the cell is so small, all sounds get massively amplified.

And I'm the kind of person who's sensitive to noises in the first place. Very often, when someone eats a packet of crisps in public, I have to walk away as the sound annoys me so much. Here, you had to endure it. You were nailed to a torture bed. Having to go through the pain of having to endure this day after day was the worst torture.

And then there was the constant sound of the TV. The TV was on all day. And what was on were always the same terrible sitcoms with canned laughter. Oh how I hated them. What I hated more were the commercials. Have you watched normal daytime TV recently? By the evening, you'll have seen the same commercial 100 times. Never in a million years would I waste my time like that, and it drove me mad that I was forced to do so.

Tinto didn't seem to mind at all. He had this ability to completely switch off his brain, leave it in the corner, and stare at the TV all day, occasionally laughing. No ambition whatsoever. No problem with the fact that his time was completely wasted. I admired that in some ways but it also annoyed me. Sometimes he almost seemed like a dumb animal to me who did nothing bit shit, eat and stare at the TV. Shit, eat, repeat. Shit, eat, repeat. I recoil just thinking about it.

The regime improved somewhat after the quarantine period, but not much. We were let out two hours in the morning and two in the afternoon. (For one hour of each the rat cage was open for exercise).

Dinner was at around 4pm, after which we were locked up for the rest of the day. That is a long evening!

The food was ok, but the portions were miniscule. Bread was rationed at 2 slices per prisoner per day, as well as the breakfast packs. You couldn't even get a whole bowl of vegetables, they gave you about half a spoon that would hardly cover the bottom of the bowl; it was ridiculous. I usually ran out of canteen by Wednesday, meaning I'd be starving for two days.

INFO: THE FOOD

Prison rule 24 states that the diet provided should be 'wholesome, nutritious, well prepared and served, reasonably varied and sufficient in quantity'.[1]

The budget the prison service has allocated is around £2.70 per prisoner per day.[2] In contrast, the Eatwell guide of the NHS sets the cost of a healthy diet at £7.48 per day.[3]

Not surprising therefore is that the food provided in prison is neither nutritious, nor is it sufficient in quantity. It is much too high in processed carbohydrates and lacking in protein, healthy fats and fresh ingredients such as vegetables and salads. In addition, the calories provided fall far short of the recommended 2500kcal for an adult male.

When I asked Bill what he thought of the food, he said: "You were hungry before the meal and hungry after. Because it's all just carbs. If there were any vegetables, they were overcooked."

His view was that the prison diet would lead to "chronic health conditions and shortened life expectancy."

So why don't prisoners starve? Quite simply, because they can buy food on the canteen. Every prisoner – and I mean everyone – buys food on the canteen to top up what the prison provides. In my case, I spent around £35 per week. I once looked through the DHL delivery list of the canteen and saw that most prisoners spend around that amount, some more. As prison wages are only around £10-£18 per week, that money has to come from somewhere.

Readers might reasonably ask whether even more money should be spent on food when a prison place already costs more than £50k a year and prison should be punishment.

I have two answers. The first is from a human rights perspective, the second purely economical.

Every prisoner has the right to access to healthcare. Most people would agree that if a prisoner falls ill, he should be allowed to receive medical treatment. Providing a diet that will lead to health problems long-term is no different from denying medical care.

Even from a purely economical perspective, it would actually cost a lot less to provide an adequate diet. The food in prison is a good example of a 'false economy' – the short-term savings have negative financial consequences in the longer term.

Here are some examples why that is the case:

1. Food waste

Much is thrown out, resulting in enormous food waste and blocked toilets, leading to high maintenance bills.[4]

2.Increased aggression and violence

There is evidence that a bad prison diet increases violence.

In a 2002 study published in the *British Journal of Psychiatry*, 231 inmates at Aylesbury Young Offenders Institution were either given vitamin, mineral and omega-3 supplements, or a placebo. After 142 days, the active group had committed 37% fewer acts of physical violence and 26% fewer offences overall compared to the placebo group.[5]

3. Negative consequences for physical and mental health

Bad physical health results in higher healthcare costs. This is the case both for healthcare costs inside the prison, as well as the costs incurred by the NHS after release.

Poor mental health leads to altercations with other inmates and officers, property damage, problems with substance abuse and an increased burden on mental health providers.

According to the NHS, there is a 25 years life expectancy gap between those in prison and the general population. Chronic health conditions are significantly higher among prisoners than in the general population.[6]

In the US – where the prison food budget is lower than in the UK – a report by the U.S. Department of Justice found that 40% of all inmates currently had a chronic health condition.[7]

4. Negative effects on rehabilitation

Poor nutrition can impair cognitive function and concentration.

A prisoner who is unwell and malnourished will not engage well with education and the courses provided in prison to address offending behaviour. Bad food can also increase irritable and low mood, depression and anxiety, which equally lead to worse rehabilitation and learning outcomes.

5. Increased risk of reoffending.

As explained, because the food provided is not enough, prisoners need to spend money on the canteen to have enough to eat.

Another prisoner I met at the Open Prison had savings when he came into prison, but left prison nearly broke, mostly to buy food. Not being able to save up your prison wages and leaving prison with no money increases the risk of reoffending and also means people are more likely to be homeless when they leave prison.

6. Increased criminality inside prison

Prisoners who do not have any outside support need to find some other way to pay for food. In most cases this means activity that is not desired and leads to more problems, as the prison wages of no more than £18 a week will not suffice when a can of tuna costs around £2 and a lot of money needs to be spent to make phone calls.

The issue is that all these collateral costs aren't as measurable as the £2.70 therefore increasing the budget is a tough sell.

'Food behind bars' is a charity founded by Lucy Vincent that seeks to improve prisoners' diet. She is working closely with prison kitchens to educate and empower, sourcing better ingredients and making better meals.[8]

According to her view, the money is definitely not enough, but what is also needed is a change of culture. The prison kitchen needs to be given more importance for a sense of pride to develop. Prison food should be seen as part of rehabilitation, and not of punishment.

Then there was the noise. The noise!

The cell doors were made of metal and the lock was so loud that every time a cell door was closed it caused a massive bang.

As it was one open wing, you'd hear every single door opening and closing, which was constantly. The noise was off the scale, a constant smashing of metal doors from morning to evening when we were locked in (after 1600hrs it got quieter obviously, unless some idiot decided to keep staging some protest and banging a chair against his cell door, which happened quite a lot).

Just as bad were the keys.

The constant jangling of the officers' bunches of keys.

I'll never carry a bunch of keys again in my life. It's a case of severe PTSD. Remember those scenes in movies where soldiers come back from Vietnam and they jump up scared to death every time a balloon pops? It's like that, just with jangling keys rather than gunshots.

It was all so stressful, like being on a battlefield every single minute of the day.

All of this you don't actually realise in the moment, because you have nothing to compare it to. You realise it afterwards, when your circumstances change. In the moment, all you can feel is that you're constantly stressed and on alert. In places like the Foreign National, you were always on guard, never had a moment when you could be calm. Outside you had the constant noise, inside you had the cell mate.

When I woke up in the morning the first thing that occupied my mind was whether I'd be able to go to the toilet that day. Imagine that's the thing that's foremost in your head. This is what these places reduce you to.

I was only able to use the toilet when Tinto was still asleep. When I was then sitting on the toilet doing my morning business I could see him sleeping right in front of me, less than a meter away. Had I stretched out my left arm, I could have stroked his head.

Every single day it was a massive relief – both literally and metaphorically – when that was done.

I COULD HAVE STRETCHED OUT MY ARM AND TOUCHED HIS HEAD

I felt degraded and violated as a human being for having to go through this. The right to toilet privacy is a human right that everyone should have, criminals included. If I'd sent the worst serial killer in the history of mankind to jail, I'd make sure he gets his own toilet. Not just because of him, but also because of what it would say about me if I didn't.

To me, this was by far the worst thing about prison. It was a violation of my basic human rights and my dignity. Degrading and humiliating.

If I could change just one thing about prison, I would make sure that every prisoner can use the toilet in private.

But what prisoners without privacy have to go through today is nothing compared to 'slopping out'.

INFO: SLOPPING OUT – A VERY BRITISH PRISON TRADITION

In-cell toilets were installed in most British prisons in the mid-1990s. Before then, you had a bucket.[9]

Yes, this is correct. Whether or not you were sharing a cell, you were given a bucket to urinate and defecate in. The bucket would sit in the cell all night, and after the cell doors opened in the morning had to be emptied into a large sink on the landing.

There was a queue of prisoners waiting to empty their buckets, waste from overflowing buckets making the floor slippery and obviously the whole wing would stink horrendously. Often, the sluice was blocked. This process was known as 'slopping out'.

The alternative was to defecate into a newspaper on the floor of your cell, wrap it up and throw the 'shit parcel' out of the window. That was the more hygienic option. One inmate had the job of walking along the building with a wheelbarrow and a shovel to collect all the parcels.[10]

Interestingly, many of the Victorian prisons that ran the separate system were originally built with in-cell sanitation, which was later taken out.[11]

The Woolf Report on the Strangeways Riot of 1990 identified the practice of slopping out as one of the reasons prisoners rioted, and made abolishing it one of its main recommendations.[12] Therefore in the 1990s in-cell sanitation was finally installed in all prison cells.[13]

I was counting the weeks and slowly starting to lose it. I was at the end of my tether. We had been told 3-4 weeks maximum to move into single cells, and now it had been almost 7 weeks.

It was on a Friday afternoon that I almost lost it. Someone had told us we'd be moving this week but then it didn't happen. That was one disappointment too many. I couldn't face having to make it through another weekend.

On the TV was the same milk commercial of a boy drinking a glass of milk that we'd seen a million times just that week when I started shouting at the TV: "It's a fuckin' glass of milk, you little shit! It's not a fuckin' orgasm, it's just milk!"

"Hey man, how stressed are you today?" said Tinto in his usual stoic tone. That annoyed me even more. How could none of this affect him? How could he be so satisfied?

I was starting to have thoughts of hurting him. Really smashing his face to bits. I usually don't have fantasies of hurting people, but that day I definitely did. I was probably also becoming delirious.

I formed this idea in my head that I'd have to ring the bell and force the officers to move me into a single cell. *'If you don't move me right fuckin' now, I'll smear all the walls with my own excrement and beat my cellmate to a pulp. You said 3 or 4 weeks. It's been nearly 7. Move me into a single cell right fuckin' now or you will regret it. People will die.'*

What I did instead – and what saved my life that day – was sit down and write all my sick fantasies onto a piece of paper. Live them out in my writing. Nothing was spared. Let it all out. My cellmate was beaten until he looked like a rotten pumpkin, the walls were full with his blood and my excrement.

And, boy, did that help. A cathartic experience. After a few pages I felt calmer. I had actually found a way of making it through the day. And through the weekend.

The next week I was moved into a single cell on the third floor. No imagining how big a deal that was. It was a massive deal, the greatest relief I ever experienced in my life.

That afternoon, a pen and a piece of paper had saved my life. It was the only thing I could have done, other than actually doing something stupid.

After the move to the single cell, things were becoming a little better. Good enough to not kill yourself or hurt anyone.

I started working as a wing painter, which I enjoyed. The good thing about it was that you only had to work every other day. I was more or less my own boss, improving the paint work of the whole wing, and doing whatever I felt was necessary to improve.

I was now also able to exercise in my cell which was a relief, as the hour running around the rat cage wasn't always enough for me.

There was also a gym, but it was always cancelled. Usually staff shortages. I once did a count. Out of 12 gym sessions over 4 weeks, 9 were cancelled. A joke.

That's something that needs to be taken into consideration. Most things that might be available in prison in theory, in practice aren't. Due to the structure of the regime and due to staff shortages.

If there are, for example, not enough staff on shift to open the cells, the prison is kept in lockdown and all activities are cancelled.

This was a regular occurrence at the Foreign National Prison.

I was now also able to physically visit the library once a week, which was another great improvement.

My friend Vinnie had sent me in a parcel with Italian DVDs. It arrived really swiftly – reception here was working much better than it had at the Training Prison.

It included "Il Commissario Montalbano" – the famous Inspector from Sicily. I watched all episodes with relish. Still one of my favourites to this day...

Here I learnt expressions such as "mi stai proprio rompendo i coglioni" and "anche potrebbe essere una mossa intelligente"

There was also Season 1 of "I bastardi di Pizzafalcone" and a Sky Series called "1992/1993/1994" about Italy in the early nineties: The fight against the mafia, political corruption (mani puliti) and the rise of Berlusconi. It was an excellent series and I watched it many times.

Having these things to watch really helped me make it through this period at the Foreign National.

You just muddled your way through. It was a lot more difficult to focus and feel positive at this prison, but being in a single cell meant it was possible to exist in some way as a human being. There was the stress of the constant noise on the wring, the metal-door-slamming, the keys jangling, the shouting, but at least in your cell in the evenings when the prison was locked down you could have some quiet.

I want to bring the focus on the prison officers a little, as I haven't talked about them much before.

It was more than obvious that they didn't have a great time, either.

What I had noticed at the hellhole is that if a prison is really bad, it's the officers that suffer the most, possibly even more so than the prisoners.

They will then also receive lots of abuse from prisoners, who fail to understand that systemic issues have nothing to do with the officers, who are only trying to do their best. The officers are just a small cog in the machinery themselves.

One officer confided in me that he hated being back from holiday and hated the place.

"Well, at least you get to go home every night, I wish I was in that position" was my reply. "Yes, but most of you leave here for good very soon. I've got to stay here for the rest of my life."

INFO: THE PRISON OFFICER

Who wants to lock up people for a living?

Without sounding disparaging, my impression was that the average prison officer was someone who didn't know what else to do in life. You didn't need a degree and it's a relatively decent and secure salary. But then that's the case for so many professions and doesn't have to be a problem. Everybody needs to do something.

And in theory you are able to make a difference in people's life's. If you can actually help offenders to turn their lives around, isn't that amazing in theory? I did feel that many officers genuinely wanted to make a difference. Unfortunately, it's the practice of what prison is like that must be so dispiriting for them.

It's an odd job, but someone has to do it. I did not find in any way that officers were sadists or enjoyed punishing people.

I have always been treated respectfully and like a human being, rather than a criminal, by officers. Sure, there was the shouting at the hellhole, but that was more the culture of the place than fault of the officers.

As mentioned above, in a bad prison within a bad prison system, it's the officers who suffer the most.

I personally thought being an officer was an awful job and I didn't envy them, nor was surprised that so many seemed to hate it. It's a dull occupation 95% of the time where all you do is open and close door, wait in the exercise yard for an hour, or answer thousands of stupid questions that would all be unnecessary if the prison service used modern technology.

You could see it with young officers who had just started.

The disillusionment and disappointment was written all over their faces.

But then it can turn from dull to very dangerous so quickly. It is a very dangerous occupation, which should not be forgotten.

It's therefore not surprising that there is a huge recruitment problem. Prisons are overcrowded and understaffed – there aren't enough officers and they are leaving in droves.[14]

My solution would be a reformed prison system that is geared fully towards rehabilitation and where officers do more than just lock and unlock doors. They would be more like social workers or mental health workers. The job would be more intellectually challenging and training would be several years, instead of just a few weeks.

It's quite simple. A better prison system would make being a prison officer a much more satisfying occupation.

I need to say that throughout my three years in prison I was always treated with respect and never like a criminal. I was able to talk to officers on the same level as you'd talk to any other human being. There never was a feeling that they were 'looking down on you'. Of course, some officers were nicer than others, just like anywhere, and some were a bit more old-school and maybe bitter after so many years.

I've never seen an officer abusing a prisoner, being violent, or punishing anyone for no reason. What I did notice at the Foreign National prison, however, is that you were treated differently by some officers depending on how foreign you were.

There was an unofficial scale of 'foreignness'.

I was lucky as I was a white western European – therefore a 'good foreigner' – at the very top of the scale, along with foreigners from the US, Canada, Australia and New Zealand (who aren't really foreigners as such).

At the very bottom of the scale were Muslims, if they looked like they could be members of Isis or the Taliban. Everyone else was in between, according to how divergent culturally from Britain.

As a result, an Indian Hindu is viewed much more positively than a Muslim Afghan. A Romanian or Pole is viewed more positively than an Albanian or Georgian, and so forth.

An example to explain what was going on was told to me by a 30-year old Spanish guy who moved to the UK when he was 2 but never obtained UK citizenship.

He'd lived in the UK all his life and had a British London accent. However, he looked somewhat Middle Eastern.

He explained to me that as soon as the officers heard him talk, they'd treat him differently – somewhat warmer and being more helpful. It did not surprise me when he told me this as I'd noticed the exact same thing in the treatment of the other prisoners.

What I do not want to say is that it was overt racism.

It didn't go that far, but what it clearly was, was a bias. It was an unconscious bias that some officers showed more than others. It's a bias that we all have to some degree, but some of us are more aware of it and make a conscious effort to balance it out, whilst others don't. And if you're in the firing line, you notice it more than if you are not.

Although I did not really make any lasting friendships at the Foreign National, as I was sharing the wing with the same people every day, and therefore I started talking to some other inmates on a regular basis. For me it was mostly the afternoon exercise session where I liked to walk around the rat cage and talk to someone. If not, I walked around the circle alone and cleared my head.

One fellow inmate that stayed in my memory was a guy from Zimbabwe who was about to be deported. He had been challenging his deportation for the last ten years and was now running out of options. His flight was scheduled for the coming Wednesday, but he was still hoping that he wouldn't be on it.

Although he did actually own a house in Zimbabwe, he didn't want to go back. He did have a wife and children here in the UK, but had been in the country illegally from the start. Therefore, he wasn't allowed to work, which meant he did all sorts of things that would keep landing him back in prison.

I found it all difficult to understand. What kind of life could you possibly have if you have no right to live or work? His situation was never going to get better. And why did he start a family under those circumstances?

I didn't know nor understand the whole story, but I found it difficult to understand why one would want to live like that. I didn't like the mentality. But then I've never been to Zimbabwe and I live in a completely different world. I just think if you move to another country, you need to have some sort of plan how that is going to work out (unless you are a refugee, which he wasn't).

Two of the 'most normal' guys on the wing were there for driving offences similar to mine.

One was from Massachusetts and getting himself deported back to the US. We had a few nice chats about politics and the world. He was tuning cars (legally) and was hired by someone to film a video for a youtube channel. When he drove extremely fast as they were filming the video, he lost control and drove into a tree.

The other guy, Oscar, was from Romania, but had been living in the UK for over ten years.

He was on the motorway and braked too hard as he was trying to turn into a lay-by, causing the truck behind him to hit another vehicle. I sometimes walked with Oscar in the afternoons and we had some good conversations. Very nice guy, but a bit crazy. He mostly ate oranges and avoided the prison food.

BUDDHISM & AA

The two things that got me out of my cell when I wasn't working were the weekly Buddhist meeting and AA. (Apart from the gym, which was always cancelled, and the library for a 15min slot)

For me Buddhism in prison was about the general positive mentality and meditation. A lifelong atheist, I didn't suddenly become a believer in prison. But if there was one religion I'd choose, it would be Buddhism.

We would meet in the church. There were usually just two or three prisoners, with myself being the only European. The Buddhist chaplain would light some scented candles and we would sit around the carpet and meditate for 25 minutes.

Afterwards, we would have a cup of tea and a chat. That to me was the best bit. Having intelligent conversations about all sorts of topics, especially with someone from the outside world was always a wonderful thing. Talking about the outside world was fantastic, because prisoners mostly just talk about prison.

I did have a good rapport with the chaplain. The only thing that annoyed me was that he would make comments when I drank a whole glass of the milk that was meant for the tea, or took some biscuits back with me to the cell.

"Imagine if everyone did this!"

He clearly didn't understand my situation. I took the biscuits because I had nothing left in my cell, canteen delivery was tomorrow and dinner wasn't going to be enough.

Would it have been too hard for him to just bring some milk in and some biscuits out of his own pocket? Surely that would have been an act of kindness.

I think the fact that I was a bit annoyed at him just shows my general agitation during this time. Things were a bit better since I had been moved to a single cell, but this baseline of general agitation and being on edge was just always there.

The best thing about going to the church to meditate and talk it was to be able to get away from the wing into a different environment for a while. It allowed you to forget about it all for an hour and recharge the batteries. We simply didn't get away from the wing often enough. Especially if you don't even have a proper exercise yard it's just incredibly claustrophobia-inducing.

The same goes for the AA meetings.

It was just lovely to sit around a table and talk for an hour with people who were in the same boat and people from the outside who were non-judgmental. You were able to share your experience and you could listen to others' experience and have some meaningful conversations. In addition, meeting some people from the outside world and having a conversation with them was so important in reminding you that there's still a world out there, even if it felt like it was light years away.

The Move

Completely unexpected, as always, the female officer opened my cell on Monday morning and blurted out: "Oh I've just heard you're leaving us!" I had no idea what she was talking about.

I pretended to myself that I hadn't heard what she had said and continued as normal. The golden rule of imprisonment is to never get your hopes up, because you will be bitterly disappointed and crushed otherwise. I decided to not make myself vulnerable.

When more officers mentioned something similar, I said I didn't know and ignored them. It was sometimes the case that officers were misinformed or that things changed from day to day.

It was only Wednesday, when the officer locking me up for the evening said, "You're on the transfer list for tomorrow morning, open prison, but keep it quiet, please,", that I allowed myself to believe it. The excitement was almost unbearable.

It had come completely unexpected, as both OMU (Offender Management) as well as Immigration had told me that I would have to spend the remainder of my sentence at the Foreign National and wasn't eligible for D-Cat Open conditions. In addition, I had actually been categorised to D-Cat, which nobody had told me. It's a good example that you could never rely on what people in authority who should know told you. It was often the case that nobody really knew what was going on.

Sleeping was difficult that night, I was excited. Could it really be true? I continued to follow the golden rule though, even until I was in the van. You never knew what might happen.

Claude, one of the nicest officers, shook my hand as he opened my door that morning and wished me all the best.

"You don't really belong here anyway," he told me.

"I do belong here, but I understand what you mean", was my answer.

That was honest, because while I always thought that I deserved to be in prison, I did not think that I deserved to be in a place like the Foreign National. Nobody deserved to be there in my opinion

CHAPTER 4: THE OPEN PRISON
A SENSE OF FREEDOM

The journey to the Open Prison was a completely new experience emotionally. Whereas the drive to the Foreign National had been filled with dread and despair, this was like the journey to Disneyland when you're 9 years old. It proves that following the golden rule – expect the worst and lots of it – really works wonders. When something good happens, it feels like a miracle.

It's worth mentioning at this point that for a British national with a similar offence going to an open prison is the normality. In fact, many move quite quickly to open conditions and spend the majority of their sentence there.

But I was a foreign national and therefore everything was different. To me this seemed unfair.

I was aware that I'd probably have to go back to the Foreign National at some point towards the end of my sentence. I'd have to go back and wait for the answer of the Home Office. And possibly, I wouldn't get the answer until my release date, meaning I'd have to stay in prison past it.

This happens routinely. I had met many foreign offenders who were still in prison beyond their release date waiting for an answer, sometimes for many months. Prisons for foreign nationals are the only ones that can hold prisoners under immigration powers after their release date. In any other prisons, they have to release them on the release day.

It was all very complicated and uncertain. Prison in itself is hard enough. But at least you know when you'll be getting out (Unless you have a life sentence). Having to deal with this immigration shit was such an additional cause of worry.

The complete uncertainty of what was going to happen was simply difficult to deal with.

I therefore tried to just push it as far away as I could. For now, I was here. And that was good.

The first thing I noticed when we arrived at the Open Prison was that there was no fence and no gate. We arrived at a roundabout; with a car-park straight ahead and a security barrier for vehicles with a gatehouse to the right. There was a row of residential houses just opposite the prison entrance.

We drove through the barrier and then took a left into another car park behind the gatehouse. After stepping out of the prison van we walked into prison reception. From inside you could see the houses on the other side of the road. If I would have wanted to, I could have done a runner to see how far I would make it...

As we were all processed through reception (whether open prison or not, your property still had to be checked and put on your property card; you were of course also issued with a prison ID) we were told we could wait on the bench in the fresh air outside.

It was lovely being able to move around without anyone monitoring your every step. The way we were treated by the officers at the reception also felt different. It was all more relaxed. Everything was just a bit more normal, more humane.

As we were sitting on the bench outside, some reception orderlies arrived. They had brought a trolley for us take our belongings to the wings and greeted us. An orderly named Albert introduced himself to me and we started chatting. He was in for a similar offence – causing death by dangerous driving. We chatted a bit, the usual small talk.

After our property was fully processed, we loaded it onto the trolley. Just as we were about to make our way up the road towards the wings, the reception received a phone call. Apparently, there was a problem with one of us – Perrati from Albania. We knew each other vaguely, but had never spoken more than a few words. Nice guy in any case. The problem was the he still had unresolved proceeds of crime case worth £70. This meant that he wasn't eligible for open conditions. The operational staff at the Foreign National must have overlooked this.

He was immediately placed into the cage at the back of reception and had handcuffs put on. Now he was awaiting the transport back to the Foreign National. What a horror!

Seeing him in that cage – the only place here that had bars! – I felt sorry for him. He looked like a shattered human being, completely broken.

When you're in prison there's not one moment when you don't expect something like this to happen. At any time someone could come and take you to a different prison.

In my case, the fear was especially strong; as I knew I was on borrowed time and would at some point be sent back to the Foreign National, just like Perrati now. For the following months, whenever I'd see officers I didn't know walking on the landing towards my cell, I'd think: 'That's it. They're coming to take me back.'

I pushed the fear as far away as I could. For now I was here.

We pushed the trolleys with our belongings up the road, still feeling sorry for Perrati. To the right we passed a fenced compound of portacabins. This is where the inmates that had outside jobs were housed. Straight ahead I was able to make out two large buildings, which I assumed must be the wings. We reached a T-junction and turned left, leaving one of the buildings behind to our right. As we followed the main road, the other building, A-wing, came into view: A rectangular reddish lego block of monstrous ugliness. What were they thinking when they built this?

At reception I was given my room keys. I was assigned a room in the induction wing on the ground floor. The room was small and just about fitted a bed, a table, a cupboard and a chair. There was a TV in the room but the telephones were on the landing. All of this mattered a lot less here, as you were never locked in your room.

THE OPEN PRISON

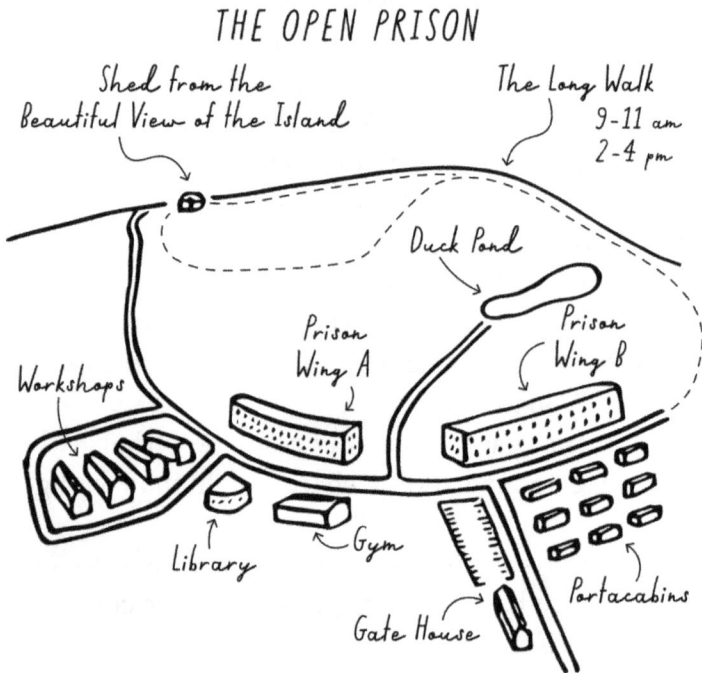

Shed from the
Beautiful View of the Island

The Long Walk
9-11 am
2-4 pm

Duck Pond

Prison
Wing A

Prison
Wing B

Workshops

Library

Gym

Gate House

Portacabins

Looking out the window I saw countryside. There was grassy hill leading up behind the wing. There were rabbits everywhere, it was wonderful to see. There were also lots of ravens, jackdaws and all sorts of other birds. Life!

Albert gave me a tour of the prison grounds.

I noticed that people were smoking cigarettes, as it was allowed to smoke here. There was also rubbish everywhere – a lot of it seemed to have been thrown out the window. Bread to feed the seagulls, which were everywhere.

We headed right after leaving our wing and I found some of the buildings I had expected to find: library, gym, workshops.

As we continued our tour by turning the other way I saw the large education building, OMU and administrative buildings, chapel, healthcare. They were all buildings you'd expect in a prison, nothing out of the ordinary. There was no prison shop. For some reason, I had imagined a shop where you could buy canteen items all day. But it wasn't the case. You still had to order you canteen on a weekly basis as in other prisons.

I was now able to walk in a straight line for several hundreds of meter, fulfilling my lifelong dream, as I had imagined it at the Foreign National.

The highlight came at the end of our excursion. We arrived at a field behind the prison grounds. "Up there is the Long Walk. You can pick up a pink band from the office and go there every day from 9 to 11 and 2 to 4. People get really fit here running up that hill."

"Can I go there tomorrow morning?"

"Of course"

"Amazing!"

I could hear a woodpecker drilling into a tree somewhere. This was nature. We headed back to the wing.

Albert explained the main prison rules to me.

There was no fence, therefore they had a roll call four times a day to check prisoner numbers and that nobody had done a runner. They locked the wings at 19.45 and opened them again at 8.30 after the first roll call, so overnight you were locked inside the wing.

"The food is alright. You get chips basically every day." He seemed to see that as a positive. As we were back at the wing, the smokers outside the building greeted me with: "Guten Tag!"

The atmosphere was so different to what I had been used to. It felt much more like some sort of a camp or army barracks than a prison.

Emotionally, the move from the Foreign National to the Open Prison very much mirrored the move from Victorian hellhole to Training Prison, except that the contrast was even starker.

Back at the wing office I was given an induction booklet and an induction passport that I had to get stamped over the next week, visiting all the different departments and signing up for work or education.

This being an open prison, I had hoped that I didn't have to work, so I could focus on my language learning and writing. I saw prison jobs mostly as a waste of time. But my worries were unfounded as, by sheer coincidence, the job that I was assigned to fit me like a glove. It was probably the only job in the whole prison that I could have actually seen myself doing, and that I was sure I would enjoy: Working in the library. I was very lucky indeed.

Library Orderly – The Best Job in the Prison World

The library here worked differently to what I was used to. In closed conditions you were given your weekly library slot of 15min when you could go to the library (If that timeslot would clash with something else, like work, gym or a doctor's appointment, you'd miss it.). You'd be escorted to the library by an officer. If you finished reading a book in your cell, you had to wait for your next week's library appointment to return it and get another one.

Here that was all different. You could go to the library anytime, as many times a day as you liked. If you didn't have work and wanted to escape the noisy wing, the library became your refuge where you could read the newspaper, browse books and have a chat. It was a lovely quiet place and sitting there behind the desk you didn't feel like you were in prison – you almost felt like you were working in a small public library.

What made the job even more appealing was the fact that the librarian from Kent Libraries was only there a few mornings a week, at other times it was us prisoners who ran it.

When it was my shift, I'd pick up the key from the office, go to the library and open up. Sometimes I'd bring a radio; when it wasn't busy I could read behind the desk. I'd browse the Kent Library Intranet database to see if books that I wanted to read were available in any of the other Kent libraries. I'd order it and 2 weeks it was there. I was also able to order some language courses. Everything that had been so excruciatingly difficult and complicated in closed conditions was suddenly so easy.

The Newspaper Wars

The other major shift in my daily life was the newspaper.

Previously I had to spend half my days asking officers if the newspaper had arrived only to receive it at 4 in the afternoon, if lucky. More often than not I'd have to read yesterday's paper.

Here, the newspapers would arrive at the gatehouse in the morning at 8 and a prisoner would collect them and take to the wings. Most fortunate for me, that prisoner was the library orderly. And even better for me, the library itself did receive a small selection of newspapers every day, mostly tabloids, but also the Guardian.

But I wouldn't know about this for quite a while because Stan, a long-haired resident of B-Wing, was running a nice little scheme.

He would collect the newspapers every morning from the gatehouse so my lazy library orderly colleagues didn't have to do the job. In exchange, he'd keep the papers for himself and he could read The Sun for free every day.

All of this only became clear when one Saturday I was trying to collect my own newspaper ('The I paper' – as always) from the wing office and the officers told me they hadn't arrived. I enquired and was eventually informed that Stan, who usually collected them, was on his town visit that day. When Small Teddy, who had become my friend on the wing (more about him later), eventually collected them from the gatehouse, he told me there were also some library papers. I looked at the papers, which had 'library' written on the address label.

"What library papers?" I said baffled. "I work at the library and we don't get any newspapers! Surely I'd know because I've been working there for over a month!"

The next time I saw Stan carrying the stack of newspapers, I intercepted him: "Are you Stan?"

"Yes, who's asking?"

"I work at the library. Do we get any newspapers for the library?"

"Yes, but I collect them for the boys there, so they let me have the the Sun as a favour."

"But they're for the library, so everyone can read them."

"Nobody reads them there, they get wasted. On the wing at least people read them."

This nonsense wouldn't stand.

I spoke to Molly, the librarian from Kent Libraries, who was there in the mornings. She had no idea about any newspapers, either. After speaking to her boss she made it clear to me that only I should be collecting the newspapers as they were for the library. She even printed me a written confirmation for the gatehouse as a confirmation and to prevent Stan from collecting the papers.

A approached Stan and explained to him that from now on, as the library orderly, I'll be getting the newspapers.

This worked well for a few days until one day, when I was at the gatehouse to collect them they were, once again, gone. Someone had already taken them. It was Stan.

What ensued was a long battle over who'd be collecting the newspapers. Despite the fact that he'd been found out and exposed as a thief, Stan simply wouldn't cede. When I spoke to the other library orderlies about it, they couldn't care less. "To be honest, nobody cares about the newspapers", was their answer.

It was about the principle. The newspapers were there for the library, so everyone could sit there and read them. They belonged to everyone, not to Stan. (Although self-interest also played a part as I would from time to time read the Guardian.) If Stan wanted to read the Sun, he could just order one for himself, like I did. Why does he actually believe he is entitled to steal someone else's newspaper? It was infuriating.

The battle continued until Stan had his first town leave, staying at approved premises (A sort of hostel for prisoners) in London. He went to the pub and came back to the hostel not being able to walk in a straight line. He was immediately sent straight back into closed conditions. After 18 years in prison he had finally made it into open conditions, so this must have been a heavy blow. He would most likely spend the remainder of his sentence in closed conditions.

Stan's departure made me the king of the newspapers. A job I would love doing every day. It became a rock solid part of my daily routine for a year.

Another library-related battle had to do with the work ethic of the other prisoners working in the library. As I have explained earlier, the library was run by us the prisoners, except when Molly was in.

I've noticed quite quickly that the library was often closed when it should have been open. In fact, unless Molly the librarian was there, or it was my shift, it was almost never open.

This wasn't just annoying for all prisoners who wanted to borrow a book; it also became a particular problem for me. As I became known to everyone for working there, they all approached me when the library wasn't open.

"Why isn't the library open?

"I'm sorry, it's not my shift."

"Why isn't the library open?"

"Sorry, it's not my shift."

It was annoying. Wherever I went, people asked me why the library wasn't open. They even knocked on my room door in the evenings. On many occasions, I even opened the library although it wasn't my shift. When I went for a run in the morning and came past the library, people came towards me, their arms full of books they wanted to return and a needy, questioning expression on their face.

This couldn't go on, I had to resolve it. So I went over to B-Wing and confronted Thomas, who had worked in the library the longest and was the main offender.

"It's not your problem. You worry about your shift, we worry about ours," was his reply.

"Of course it's my problem. It becomes my problem when everyone's asking me all day, when people knock on my door when I'm not working: 'Why's the library not open? Why's the library not open?' It's annoying, man!"

"That's part of the job."

And then he launched a counterattack, accusing me of asking people to file complaints against him (which was true). There was no point in continuing this conversation. He didn't get it. Some people live in a different universe. Still, I was fuming inside. What was wrong with this guy?

Eventually I had no other choice but to tell Molly, who promised to do something about it. Unfortunately, Thomas was not sacked from his job, but was released anyway a few months later.

But because I had made Molly aware of the problem, many more library orderlies were hired over the next few weeks. Better ones, too. Meaning that very soon, all of it stopped being a problem. The library was always open, and the newspapers were always on the table. And that had mostly been my achievement.

Prison isn't a place to make friends. Any friends you make might be moved to a different prison tomorrow, and you won't ever see them again. You see someone every day – your cell neighbour, your co-worker at the library, the guy who has the same gym sessions – and then one day they're suddenly gone. And later in the day someone else lives in their cell, as if they hadn't existed.

I understood that from the beginning and I wasn't there to make friends. I had goals of what I wanted to achieve and I was pursuing those, keeping to myself. What is the point of spending all day talking to people you'll never see again, just to kill the time? That doesn't mean that I was an unfriendly hermit who wouldn't talk to others, it just means that I had other priorities. And I wanted to stay away from the politics and the drama. I just didn't care about gossip and stories about new prisoners who had just arrived on the wing. It was too small a world for me.

At the Training Prison of course I would combine my afternoon walk with a nice talk, but once it was time to go back inside I'd do something in my cell rather than standing in the corridor talking about nothing. Or, let's say nothing worth talking about.

In addition, there just weren't that many people you could have a meaningful conversation with. That doesn't mean there weren't any at all, just not many.

It didn't stop to amaze me how people could sit around a table talking shit at 7 in the morning and by 8 in the evening they'd still be sitting there on the same chair, still talking shit. Just to 'kill the bird'. Not a very effective bird-killer in my opinion, especially if you consider the sort of conversations they were having all day. If you listened in by accident, you wanted to either shout: "You morons!" or run away over the hills.

I was just staying away from it all. Apart from some people I got on with here and there, such as Bill, with whom I am still in contact. But then we were both oddities in prison.

There were two sides as to how I saw myself in relation to the other inmates. On the one hand, I was just like them and fit in perfectly.

I was a messed up idiot who had made stupid decisions and horrible mistakes in his life, but who had never intended to cause anyone harm.

But on the other hand I stood on the sidelines, observing everything from the outside. I was an observer more than a participant, not a part of the prisoner community (if there was such a thing).

The biggest different between open and closed conditions socially is the mingling. In closed conditions you will spend anything between 23 and 18 hours alone locked in your cell. You spend the evenings alone in your cell. Here, the wing was open all evening. People were playing cards or board games, did cooking, and ate together; or just hung out. All of this was of course a lot nicer than sitting alone in your cell in the evenings, but only if you had the right company.

Ron was a drug dealer from up north.

He had his room in the very corner of the wing – a secluded area far from the noise. There were always a few chairs pulled out and people having a chat. In the evenings he always had a nice circle of people around his room and one day he invited me to join in.

Over the next few weeks I'd spend quite a few evenings with the group chatting and getting to know everyone. It was a nice group.

It was one of the few occasions in prison where I came to know a small group of people a little bit better, and made some – if superficial – connections.

Ron was a smart guy with sound opinions. You could have great conversations with him. At the same time, he openly admitted that he wasn't honest, and that he was a career criminal. (At least in mentality, that's how he put it. I'm not sure I agreed, though. I was certain that he'd find his way outside after release and would never see the inside of a prison again.)

These were all nice, normal people. At the same time, some of their crimes were absolutely horrendous. One stabbed his brother in the neck with a steak knife and almost killed him; the other threw his son down a balcony.

And that's the thing you find in prison. The crime doesn't match up with the person you have in front of you.

What conclusion to draw from this depends on your world view.

Does it mean you can never trust a book by its cover and that people aren't who they present themselves to be? Or is it that anyone, even the nicest person, can have a moment of madness?

I've come to believe during my time in prison that it's neither of the two. Human psychology is too complex to categorise people and to have a universal rule of how people are.

The noise level on the wing of course was a problem. There was this constant banging that drove me mad. I couldn't figure out what it was, then I realised it was the doors themselves. People were slamming them like crazy every time they walked in and out of their rooms. And when they had their windows open it would create a strong draft that would slam the door shut.

It was partly a fault in design and the abysmal state of the building – the doors were just a lot louder than they needed to be. But it was also just that people didn't care. The slamming was sometimes so loud that when I was lying in my bed I could feel the whole building shake. I started to identify the slammers and judged people by whether they were a door-slammer or not. Whether you were a door-slammer or not said a lot about the kind of person you were in general, I was convinced.

The shouting was a similar problem.

I just didn't understand why people needed to shout all the time. There was a constant shouting on the wing with no reason for it.

A shout has one purpose only: You want to warn someone; or you need to get someone's attention in an exceptional situation. A pedestrian is looking at their phone and about to be hit by a car. This is a situation where a shout is appropriate.

You get robbed, kidnapped or you are locked in a freezer. Then you shout. If you, however, need to communicate normally with people on a daily basis, you don't shout. If someone is at the other end of the wing you walk over there and then talk to them. There's absolutely no reason to shout. These are the utter basics of civilised behaviour. Why would you shout?

It's not even worth mentioning the queue jumpers. Small Teddy had a little trick. The sink was situated close to the servery and thereby next to the front of the queue. He would wash his plate and then walk straight to the servery, jumping the entire queue.

If you have seen 'Orange is the new black' you will be familiar with the turd-in-the-shower incident. In the series, an investigation was launched into why someone kept defecating into the showers and it was found out that someone was bringing in drug into the prison which they were hiding inside their rectum. They used the shower floor so they could easily retrieve the package.

Well, the exact thing happened at the Open Prison, as if taken straight from the script of the successful Netflix series. It happened several times over a few weeks, and every time they had to bring in a guy in a hazmat suit to clean the entire toilet and shower area.

My theory was that it happened for the exact same reason as in OITNB. Ron agreed, but he mused that if he were to do the same thing, he'd lay a black bin bag underneath and then roll up everything and throw it in the bin.

There was an alternative theory that it had to do with steroids. Many of the guys here were taking steroids and, apparently, it could make you lose control of your bowel functions. So you're having a shower thinking you need to fart and – oopsy daisy. That theory didn't seem very likely to me.

In any case, when the showers weren't full of shit, the communal toilets most certainly were. There was shit all over them, a lot of the time. And nobody would clean them. Because of how labour was organised, there simply wasn't an incentive for any of the cleaners to do it. It was disgusting.

Every now and then, when I couldn't take it anymore, I took some gloves, lots of bleach and cleaned them. Others occasionally did the same. Some of the cleaners actually did their work, but most didn't. There were 40 cleaners on the wing but only around 5 of them did any work. For £10 a week there simply was no incentive to do such dirty work.

Apart from being disgusting and full of shit, there also weren't enough toilets. Each landing had no more than three cubicles for 20 prisoners. Surely they could have done with 5 when they built the place? But then again you go to prison in Thailand, and 40 people share a cell with one toilet in the corner (according to what I read in a letter sent to the Prison Reform Trust). Or even worse, with a hole in the floor in the middle, so things could have been worse.

I much preferred the communal toilets, which offered some privacy, to having to do my business in front of my cellmate.

What struck me about all the prison diaries that I've read is that the toilets are hardly ever mentioned, even though they are probably one of the most distressing aspects of prison life. Jeffrey Archer wrote about every miniscule thing he did minute by minute, stretching his daily routine over three volumes, but did not once write about going to the toilet.[1] But then he did always have a single cell, so maybe it wasn't an issue for him...

I've never talked about toilets so much in my life, but there is simply no way to give an accurate account of what prison is like without mentioning them.

INFO: WORK IN PRISON

Question: When is full employment not full employment?

Answer: When it's full employment in prison.

Prisons do not produce anything. They are essentially massive dorms with a wall around them. However, prisons operate a policy of 'full employment', i.e. every prisoner needs to have a full-time job.

Do you recognise the problem? For obvious reasons, jobs need to be fabricated. At the Open Prison, there were 80 wing cleaners, but hardly any of them did any cleaning at all. The £10 weekly pay simply wasn't an incentive to many. In addition, with such high numbers of cleaners, nobody had to take responsibility and it was hard for officers to supervise effectively and keep an overview.

Were the prison service to abandon the policy of full employment, however, it would be possible to sack 60 idle cleaners and keep 20, paying them £40 a week each.

£40 per week would be much more of an incentive to work. 20 would also be a number of prisoners that could be managed and supervised more effectively. As a result, abandoning the 'full-employment' policy would result in more actual employment and a cleaner prison, including cleaner toilets. In addition, because full employment wouldn't be prescribed, it would be easier to sack people if they didn't do their jobs.

I had met a frustrated officer who had done exactly that: He had paid some prisoners more and sacked others. It worked much better, the wing was cleaner. But he was soon told that he wasn't allowed to do this and had to follow prison regulations.

Now he's given up on trying and the wing looks the way it does.

Most jobs in prison have very little to do with preparation for work in the real world. If you're a cleaner, for example, you're not being taught how to clean effectively in a professional setting. You are just given a mop and a bucket. Then you do some cleaning or not. It's all a bit pointless and unstructured.

If you work in the gardens you will not learn any skills that would prepare you for a career in gardening. Of course you are mowing the lawns, trimming the hedges, and so forth. But it's mostly just so you're occupied doing something, rather than having a structure that really looks at teaching you skills.

It's similar for all the other jobs. Some are better, some less so.

Every department has orderlies. Again, many of these orderly jobs are simply fabricated because jobs need to be given out, so they are not actually needed.

Then there are peer mentor jobs, which definitely are some of the better ones, as you're helping others.

My job as a Forward Trust mentor is a good example. There are many Shannon's Trust mentors that teach others how to read.[2] They fill such an important gap.

Other positive examples are the workshops.

I have met many prisoners that were quite happy with their work in a workshop, such as carpentry or printing.

There are also different kinds of orderly jobs for every department. Again some of these are better than others and most are fabricated.

But these exceptions are far in between. Most prison jobs are simply a waste of time, not really that much different from hanging around in your cell.

The picture on jobs in prison is therefore mixed. There are some great exceptions, but they constitute the minority.

As an environment, open prison was closer to normal life than a normal closed jail.

I once read that in daily life, you have to make around 2000 tiny decisions. In prison, this was reduced to 200, as most of your life was completely controlled. In open conditions, it would probably be closer to 500, or even more. It therefore gave you a better idea of how inmates would behave, were they back in society. You saw the true nature of how people really were; which I often found very irritating.

One day, when I was at the library and especially irritated I ranted: "I hate prisoners! They're all idiots! If everyone in the UK would be like the people in here, Britain would be a third-world country!"

One person agreed, but another one asked me: "What have you done to be here?"

"Causing death by careless driving" I replied.

"Terrible! That poor family..." he said to me accusingly.

101

He had put me in my place. My impression was that he thought I saw myself as better than anyone else and therefore wanted to give me a reality check. It certainly worked. I felt humbled, guilty and ashamed.

Was I deluded? Did I live on a different planet? There's not a moment in which I don't have this doubt about my perception of things.

Salim - A case of severe mental health problems

Salim looked like he couldn't hurt a fly. He was pathologically shy. Which made his crime all the more surprising. He had stabbed a 'Just eat' delivery guy in the chest with a knife.

Why he would do such a thing was a mystery at this point, but would become a lot clearer once I got to know Salim better.

The reason we became known to each other was not just because he lived a few doors down from me, but also because he started working in the library.

He became my ally when it came to shift shirkers, and we slowly became friends, always making sure all shifts were covered, and often working the same shift, talking. He would bring his little radio, and we would have nice conversations; either with each other or with other people who were sitting in the library.

Over time, especially with the introduction of the newspapers, the library had become a refuge from the noise and drama of the wing. You could read the paper and have a nice chat.

Salim had a tendency to over-share information: He told me that the doctor had put his finger up his rectum to check his prostate and also that he kept a container in his cell, so he didn't have to walk to the bathroom ten times a night, as he had a weak bladder.

He had a big crush on the Princess of Wales and every time she would be in the papers (which was basically all the time as we had The Sun, the Mirror and the Mail) he'd say: 'Look at her! Look at my Catherine! Isn't she so beautiful?'

When it came to our conversations we agreed on some things, although arguments sometimes became heated due to the fact that we were both stubborn and convinced we were right. But most of his views were a bit odd, to say the least. He was deeply religious and convinced that the fact that the earth revolves around the sun and that the day has 24hours proved the existence of God. When I challenged him on it and said that what he called proof proved absolutely nothing and that there existed no proof of the existence of God whatsoever, a long heated argument ensued.

He also believed that the Freemasons controlled everything and that all world leaders were puppets. I asked him to explain the difference between the Freemasons and the Illuminati.

Most of his views were completely contradictory. For example, he said that the Freemasons were Jews who controlled everything, but he was also convinced that Islam was invading the West, controlling everything and usurping us from underneath.

When it came to more practical questions, such as diet (he constantly complained about health issues, so I recommended that he eat more healthily and buy some fruit and vegetables on the canteen) he would usually agree, only to disagree one week later.

And then agree again the next week, only to then fall back on his original position. In our discussions, we usually came to some sort of conclusion or agreement, just for the conversation to start from zero again the next time we had a shift. We were basically having the exact same discussions every week, without moving one inch towards a resolution."I'm very set in my ways" he'd sometimes admit.

Although he was completely convinced his conspiracy theories were the truth, what he did understand, and often said to me, was that he had mental health problems. But I don't think he understood the full extent and I don't think he was able to determine what exactly his problem was. I thought he might have been a paranoid schizophrenic. He thought people were after him. He once came to my cell, outraged: "He took my cupboard! The officer just came to my cell and took my cupboard! He's got it with me!"

I told him: "Well, you had two cupboards, didn't you? All the other cells have one. Look at my cell, I've got one."

He was often convinced that officers were singling him out or that people were having a grudge against him.

He was pathologically paranoid. Which I thought might explain his crime. He was convinced the delivery guy – who often came to the house to deliver to the neighbours – was an agent of some secret organisation who was spying on him and ultimately intended to kill him. Therefore he had to take the first preventative step, by stabbing him several times in the chest. At least that's the story that I made up in my mind, trying to find an explanation.

Salim also had an inner rage that his outward demeanour completely betrayed. "Look at these idiots! They're like apes dangling from that bar!" He'd rant when he saw people exercising behind the library. "If you want to exercise, go to the gym!"

"Well, there are only three gym sessions a week, that's not enough for many." I explained.

"Only idiots go to the gym!"

He would rant and rant about people who were different from him.

"Just let them do whatever they want; they're not doing us any harm, are they?'

"Yes, you're right." he'd say, just to continue ranting five minutes later.

I also sometimes thought that he was a bit racist. He'd complain about racism against Indian people, but when it came to Black people, it was suddenly a different story.

It needs to be said that we did get along and I'm sure that he wished me well. But when it came to how he saw many other people, or people in general, I'm not so sure. He didn't seem to like people very much in general. I do wish him well and I'm grateful we had those days in the library.

How will he do when he gets out? I don't know. I'm suspecting he'll always have some sort of issues. Salim is an example of someone who would have needed intense mental health support. He needed a level of support that unfortunately just didn't exist. I do know that he did receive some support at a previous prison, but here there wasn't even a therapist. The only help came in form of an officer who served as a counsellor.

It's such a wasted opportunity. The many years in prison would have been the ideal time to address his mental health issues. Addressing these issues could have also mitigated his risk of reoffending. After release it will be much more difficult for, with all the challenges that life brings with it.

Small Teddy

Another character, and a real character, was Teddy. He was probably my favourite person on the wing. Already in his 70s, he had been to a Borstal when he was a teenager, and spent his life being in and out of prison. He was highly intelligent. Very interested in nature, he'd point out all the different birds and plants to me when we went for a walk.

"Last year, in that tree, there was a long-eared owl nesting. It's not here this year." He mentioned the long-eared owl on several occasions. I would sometimes ask him how prison used to be in the 80s and 90s. He explained that the food was much better. The breakfast in particular with cooked porridge and scrambled eggs. It wasn't a breakfast pack like today, but an actual meal. But he wouldn't usually like to talk about his past. What interested him most were the birds and the gardening.

He also grew his own vegetables. When he had home leaves, he'd ask me to water his plants. In turn, when I couldn't do the newspapers, I'd ask Teddy to do them. He would read the Telegraph every day, but only to do the crosswords. So I'd try to make sure he got the Telegraph every day.

He was also a vegan, probably the only one on the wing. Heck, let's face it, probably the only one in the prison. I had been also been a vegan throughout my time at the Training Prison, but over here I was struggling with it. The vegan meals were just awful. Every tiny bit of protein was replaced with carrots. Everything was full with carrots, every day. A bean casserole would be a carrot casserole.

One time it annoyed me so much that I knocked on the Governor's door and showed it to him. I asked him whether he saw any beans in that bean casserole.

"There's a bean here", he said. "Oh wait, no, it's actually a piece of corn."

INFO: FOOD - CALORIES PROVIDED & PLASTIC USED

Following up on the previous info-box on food, here are examples of meals provided with the correspondent calories, as I thought it would be nice to see what is actually served. As I wasn't able to weigh every single ingredient with a scale, the calories are estimates.

Option 1: Chicken
Breakfast: 200kcal
- 189ml carton of milk: 80kcal
- Daily allowance of 1x 30g pouch of oats: 120kcal

Hot Lunch: 850kcal
- Roasted chicken leg: 350kcal
- Side of white rice: 400kcal
- Bowl of boiled diced carrots: 100kcal

Cold Dinner: 170kcal
- 2 boiled eggs: 120kcal
- Iceberg lettuce, 3 slices of tomato & cucumber each, no dressing: 50 kcal

Total: 1220 kcal

Option 2: Fish
Breakfast: 200kcal
- 189ml carton of milk: 80kcal
- Daily allowance of 1x 30g pouch of oats: 120kcal

Hot Lunch: 850kcal
- Very small piece of white fish, 60g with sauce: 150kcal
- Side of roast potatoes: 500kcal
- Bowl of peas & sweet corn: 200kcal

Cold Dinner: 250kcal
- 1 can of sardines: 200kcal
- Iceberg lettuce, 3 slices of tomato & cucumber each, no dressing: 50 kcal

Total: 1300 kcal

Option 3: Vegetarian Option
Breakfast: 200kcal
- 189ml carton of milk: 80kcal
- Daily allowance of 1x 30g pouch of oats: 120kcal

Hot Lunch: 650kcal
- Bean casserole (Red Kidney Beans, Carrots & Potatoes): 200kcal
- Side of boiled potatoes: 350kcal
- Bowl of mixed vegetables: 100kcal

Cold Dinner: 150kcal
- Mixed Beans & Potatoes: 100kcal

- Iceberg lettuce, 3 slices of tomato & cucumber each, no dressing: 50 kcal

Total: 1000 kcal

Plastic waste

The plastic waste in prison is gigantic.

I've already mentioned the breakfast packs. Individual tiny 30g portions of cereals wrapped in plastic, then surrounded by a second layer of plastic.

The cold meal, rather than being served on plates like lunch, is equally all packed in small plastic containers. Then there are the small wrappers of crisps, chocolate bars, etc.

I have calculated that the prison service could – apart from saving money – save over 150 million pieces of plastic packaging a year by:

1. Getting rid of the awful breakfast packs and replacing them with weekly rations of oats, nuts and tea/coffee in paper bags.
2. Serving the cold meal on a plate similar to lunch.
3. Getting rid of the crisps/chocolate bars and instead increasing the quality and quantity of the cold meal. When I did a survey at the open prison, all prisoners asked were in favour of this. Chocolate can be bought on the canteen. Prisoners would rather have better meals.

Teddy was very skinny and he was getting skinnier over time. Towards the end, nearing his release, scaringly so. I always put it down to the vegan food. Only after his release, when someone told me, did I find out the real reason. He had been taking heroin every single day apparently and popping all sorts of other pills. I would have never guessed.

The Language Course Fiasco

The Open Prison gave me the opportunity to really advance my language learning. As mentioned, I was able to access the entire Kent Libraries catalogue to see if there were any language courses. It wasn't much, but it was a lot more than I had before. Michel Thomas, the legendary language teacher, was my man. At some point I had his CD course for Italian, French and Spanish in my cell. We also had a collection of DVD box sets in the library and I picked all the ones that had foreign language synchronisation tracks, which allowed me to practice comprehension, and my pronunciation by repeating out loud what was said.

The fact that I was learning three languages worked to my advantage. Sometimes a series had the French audio track, sometimes it was Spanish. Along with reading, this was pretty much what I did in my cell every evening. This gave me a solid routine.

There were also PCs in the education building that I could use. They had no internet access, but Microsoft word, which meant that I could start putting together my handwritten diaries and put them into a digital format and start putting together a book.

I also ordered another language course via the Prison Education Trust, this time French. In fact, I had already filled in an application form at the Foreign National, but the education department had failed to send it off. I only found out months later.

So I did the application process again and when the course finally arrived at the prison, it was somehow lost in the mailroom. It had been delivered, as there was photographic evidence, but then it didn't manage to make its way from mailroom to education building. As the PET had paid for it, it was more difficult to get a replacement. Months had passed in the meantime, but it didn't matter as much, as I had other materials.

Kolarsky

All the other guys that had been on the van with me to arrive from the Foreign National were released by now. Two were released straight out the door from here without any immigration issues, which gave me hope. One unfortunate guy, however, had been dragged back to the Foreign National the day before his release date. His family was expecting him to be back home and instead he was sent back to the Foreign National. I'm sure the cruelty of it wasn't by design, but by the backlog of cases the home office deals with, still, it was simply cruel. Here came the fear again. This was what was in store for me.

Then, one day, an old acquaintance, Kolarsky showed up on the wing to my surprise. He told me how things had worsened in terms of overcrowding at our old home. They had now started to also double up the single cells on the first floor, increasing the capacity of the prison.

He often cooked and showed up at my door with an unexpected dinner. Really nice of him. We did go for a walk a few times, but never really became that close.

After a few months his cell was suddenly empty again. I asked someone what had happened.

"They took him back to the Foreign National."

Here it comes again....the fear.

The Long Walk

If I had to design a brochure of the Open Prison the main attraction to be advertised would be without question the Long Walk.

It was the hilly field behind the prison that we had access to from 0900 hrs to 1100 hrs and 1400 hrs to 1600 hrs every day if we collected and wore a pink band. From the top of the hill, on a nice day, you could see almost the entire Island. One lap around was around 700, 800 meters. My record became 20 rounds in just under 2 hours. But I usually didn't count; it was just for the joy of it.

The Long Walk gave me the daily break and time away from everything that was so badly needed. It was a time to clear my head by being out in nature.

THE LONG WALK – A 2 HR BREATHER TO RECHARGE THE BATTERIES AND STAY SANE

I had established a firm routine.

I'd wake up around 06.30, have coffee and do some language learning using my CDs before the opening of the front doors at 8.30am. Then I'd collect the newspapers and take them to the library. From 9 to 11 the Long Walk for a run.

Then I'd read the newspaper in my room and have lunch. After lunch I'd usually work in the library. If not, I went for the Long Walk again, this time for a walk to clear my mind, or to chat if someone else was there. Then the education building to do some writing, then dinner. In the evenings I'd read or watch my DVDs. And that was the day. Not too bad, really. But it was crucial to have a routine.

When I had a horrible stomach bug for a few days and therefore couldn't follow it, I struggled. There was nothing worse than just hanging in your room all day, it was depressing.

During the winter, when the Long Walk was closed, it was a lot harder. I found running up and down the main road boring.

Sounds spoiled considering I was in prison? It's interesting how you adapt your expectations based on what you have. Compared to closed conditions, running in a straight line for 400 meters along that main road was a dream. But compared to the Long Walk it was rubbish.

Many readers reading about the Long Walk and all my other activities will want to shout: "This isn't prison! Stop this nonsense!"

But trust me, it is still prison. It is not easy to make it through the day in prison, and you need things like the Long Walk to keep your sanity. Do not be fooled by how comfortable this all sounds. Do not underestimate how hard being locked away from life really is, whether you are able to enjoy some daily comforts or not. The only difference is that with the constant stress in closed conditions you will suffer mental health consequences over time, whereas here you could to a degree keep your sanity.

ROTL (Release On Temporary License)

Because I had found my routine and was relatively content (A 'happy prisoner' once again!), I hadn't given my first day out on temporary release much thought. I was in no rush.

Sure, I was excited about it, but at the same time I knew that having a few days out wouldn't change the fact that I'd be in prison for another year.

The day came after I had been here for four months.

In preparation, you had to get the area and the address that you wanted to go to approved. That's why it took a few months until you were let out. They needed to know that you would behave in open conditions, and they also had to get your chosen areas approved and the address provided checked by the police. As address, I chose Bill's home in Sussex after discussing it with him. The other area I chose was Stratford, as there was a direct train.

There are many things in life that don't live up to the hype, but having your first day outside of prison after some years definitely does. There's this sense of wonder and this euphoria; it's like you're a teenager who sees the big city for the first time. Everything that had once been so familiar seems exciting and new. Unfortunately, the feeling wears off quite quickly once you're used to it.

I was meeting my friends Guy and Adam on my second or third day out and I remember how nice it was to just go for a walk. We were walking from Stratford Station via the Olympic Park and Hackney Wick to Victoria Park.

"Where do you want to eat?"

"I don't care, everywhere is amazing."

Everything and everywhere was amazing.

We sat down to eat a pizza near Mile End. I had artichokes for the first time in years.

On my days out I usually went for long walks.

On my second Saturday out I walked from Stratford to Canary Wharf. I bought an Icelandic Skyr yoghurt from Tesco and sat down by the River Lea Canal opposite the Three Mills Film Studio. I hadn't had proper yoghurt in over two years. It was glorious.

During one of my walks through East London I stopped at a pub (you were allowed inside pubs if they served food) because I really fancied a non-alcoholic beer. I bought a bottle of Lucky Saint. As I nearly finished the bottle I looked at the label and realised it had 0.5% alcohol. I panicked completely, didn't finish the bottle and ran outside. There was no way the breathalyser back at the prison would have picked this up, especially after a few hours. But it made me nervous, and I felt only calmer once I was back in my room. A Lucky Saint probably has no more alcohol than the average banana. Still, to me this clearly seems to be a case of false advertising.

For my first home leave, Bill had offered me to stay at his house, as I had nowhere to go in London. All of my friends had family or lived with their girlfriend. It just wasn't practical and I didn't want to propose, especially as it was going to be every month.

It was a big ask and such a kind offer. Bill lived down near the coast between Lewes and Brighton. I had to take the train into London and then change at Victoria. At the station I tried the beyond burger at Burger King as it was new to me.

I bought two big bags of groceries with me (plenty of Skyr yoghurt and spinach. All the wonderful the stuff you could not get in prison) and small flowers for Lyndsey, his wife. Will collected me at the station.

He asked me what I wanted to do. I said I wanted to go running a lot, watch Disney+ and maybe go to the cinema. The first evening we watched the 'Banshee of Inisherin' with Colin Farrel and Brendan Gleeson.

The next morning I woke up at 4am because I was so excited.

I made a coffee in the kitchen and ventured outside, exploring the area in the dark, with the intention of running along the small canal towards Lewis. I got completely lost. Somehow I made it back and then ran the other way towards the sea. Over the next few days I went for ever more ambitions runs, often for hours, running along the coast on the top of the cliffs. I also had my phone now so I could listen to music and all my old audio books.

In the afternoons we'd have conversations in the living room – our political views aligned. Sometimes we'd go somewhere in the afternoon, maybe a walk in Lewes, maybe some shopping. In the evening we watched Disney+ or AppleTV. We saw 'the Dropout' with Amanda Seyfried – I had read the book in the library – and 'dopesick'. Both things that I really wanted to see, and they were both sublime series. I had spent years reading about these and similar series that I couldn't watch in the paper; now I was finally able to.

Having to go back to prison was of course a bit of a downer, but you could look forward to next month. It was, in any case, a real privilege. What was possibly even more important was that it allowed you to sort certain things out, such as reopening a bank account.

After my second outing at Bill's, my OMU case worker called me to her office.

"I don't even know how to say this", she started, smoking a cigarette outside the OMU building.

My immediate thought was that it had something to do with Immigration. I had to go back!

"You have a new probation worker, and she doesn't want you to have any more home leaves."

"Ehm, ok. And did she say why?"

"She thinks it's a distraction because your friend is not in London and she wants you to focus on your resettlement in London. She thinks Bill is a distraction."

"That doesn't even make any sense", I said "I can focus on my resettlement at Bill's. I have my own room, a laptop and internet access."

"Yeah, it doesn't make any sense to me either, but there's not really much we can do. You'll still have your days out to Stratford."

She was very annoyed about it and I appreciated that.

I sort of understood the decision, but I also didn't. In any case I didn't think too much about it and accepted it. I had had the experience and now had only half a year left. I'd focus on stuff in here.

I also realised another thing, which was that after those days out, coming back to prison became harder and harder. I didn't want to live just for those few days once a month, it's simply too much of a tease and too depressing.

There are many who get to go out two or even three years before their release date. That's very difficult in many ways because you can see the world outside, but your life is still on hold. You cannot make any plans for a life outside. If you have a family you are essentially a guest in your own house. You are reliant on your wife to pay for everything, unless you have a job whilst in prison, which not many do.

It is a privilege and it is so vital for being able to reintegrate into society, especially if you've been inside for a long time. But there are downsides to it.

My later days out to Stratford were compromised by the fact that there were constant train strikes. That means I often couldn't go to Stratford, but was stuck here, going to the closest town. I mostly went for long walks, often along the river through the countryside. Sometimes I went to the cinema at the local town.

Towards the end of my sentence those days out became less and less enjoyable and even started feeling like a bit like a cruel tease. I bought some cigarettes that I kept in my locker and had some cigarettes on my days out. I think I needed to make it some sort of event, give me some reward. I also from time to time smoked a cigarette inside, but I realised how nervous and agitated it made me, so I left it.

But overall I have the fondest memories of the days I was able to leave the prison. Especially the two times at Bill's; it was just very special.

Planning for Release

My release date was getting nearer.

One month before it, I was allowed to go to Brent to see my probation worker in person. This was after a previous video call with her. As I walked through Harlesden, I bumped into another prisoner I knew. You'd be surprised how many ex-prisoners walk the streets of London...

I showed my probation worker a printed piece of paper with all the plans I had made. A precise budget, and a time table.

I had printed a long list of bookshops and health shops that I was going to apply to. The bookshop idea probably came from working in the library. The other idea was working as a bicycle courier.

My idea of what the world of work was going to be like was somewhat naive. Not only did I believe it was going to be easy to find work, I also thought that these jobs were all going to be the bee's knees. My general idea of what life was going to be like after release was romantic, to say the least.

Even though I constantly reminded others how difficult release would be, at that the first weeks and months out of prison would potentially be more difficult than prison itself, when it came to myself, I couldn't help thinking it was all going to be plain sailing.

I spoke to re-settlement, who were offering to try to find me somewhere to stay on release. For that, I needed to claim Universal Credit, which I was first reluctant to do out of pride. But speaking to my probation worker it became clear that I would shoot myself in the foot not doing so, so I changed my mind. Not claiming Universal Credit means you're also not entitled to housing.

My probation worker explained to license conditions to me.

There was very little, apart from the standard: Don't break the law, don't do drugs, don't behave in an unsocial manner, stay at the same approved address, inform probation of address change or change of work situation, attend all probation meetings. Don't leave the country without prior permission.

I asked my probation worker whether I'd be allowed to drink alcohol. She laughed. "Of course, you've been in prison for three years." I had been worried about this due to my offence. My plan wasn't to go on a bender, but it would be nice to see what a beer feels and tastes like. On my days out, I often walked past pubs and thought: 'It would be lovely.'

Arrangements were also to be made for my accommodation. I'd have to go to Brent straight from prison and would be assigned somewhere to stay, therefore wouldn't be homeless.

*

Everything was set for my release.

Then, unexpected as always and a few days before the big day, an officer approached me as I came back from the Long Walk.

"Oh, Mr. Schramm, I was looking for you. I need to talk to you, let's go to the office."

It was an officer that I got along very well with. But there was something weird about her demeanour, something was off. She looked worried.

"Unfortunately, your IS91 has come through."

"You're held under immigration powers and have to go back to the Foreign National prison."

I had to take it in and wasn't immediately able to process the shock. Packing my stuff, I was struggling. I had to ask to get a glass of water and when the officer asked me if I wanted to take my little Buddha statue, I told her: "No, I've lost my faith."

Everyone was kind and the governor shook my hand, saying that he was sorry to see me go. I asked whether the IS91 was a deportation order – I knew that it wasn't – trying to cling on to some certainty or hope. Everything was up in the air now.

At reception I was strip searched and handcuffed. I was now a full criminal again.

The van had broken down, so we went via car; myself and three officers. I was handcuffed to one of the officers, sitting in the middle of the back seat. They were respectful and kind as always, but it was annoying to see how for them this was all normal. To me it didn't feel normal. It was the end of the world.

CHAPTER 5: BACK TO WHERE YOU BELONG – THE FOREIGN NATIONAL, PART 2

THE NIGHTMARE

I still knew the officers at reception, which I found surprising. Why I don't know, it had only been a year. But it felt longer.

"It's got to be harsh coming back here after a year in open conditions", one of the officers remarked.

The other officer, who knew me and was one of the best ones, told me that they would put me up in a single cell. What a silver lining that was.

Walking from the reception to the wing I noticed how clean everything was. No litter lying around, like I was used to. Of course there was no litter, as nobody would be hanging around out here; still, the contrast was stark. I noticed that a large patch of land in the middle of the prison that used to be wasteland had been nicely made up and turned into flowerbeds.

The next morning I was back in the rat cage walking around a circle. I just couldn't do it. There was no energy to run. Nor did I have the will to exercise in my cell. As I had just missed canteen, I didn't have any food, either. However, there was a box of breakfast packs in the landing so I took loads to my cell and stuffed myself.

The wing seemed even more noisy and crowded. The nationalities of most prisoners had changed. More Eastern Europeans, fewer Hispanics and Muslims. The food was significantly worse. The vegetables had been replaced with baked beans, the entire meal was now ultra-processed.

I did not handle the new situation well. Not at all, I was completely down in the dumps. My mind was a fog and I wasn't able to even try to do anything productive.

When I spoke to my mom, she said the way I was being treated was 'menschenverachtend', which roughly translated as showing disdain and contempt towards humanity.

What was likely to happen now is that I'd have to apply for 'immigration bail'. This means that I'd be released into the community until the home office had made their decision. The conditions of my release under immigration bail would be that I'd have to wear an ankle tag, have a fixed pre-approved address and won't be allowed to work or receive benefits.

This wouldn't change until the home office had made their decision, which could be months away.

I started to regret the decision not to be deported back to Germany and was for the first time convinced I had made a mistake. What had I been thinking? Immigration bail is a nightmare of the worst kind imaginable.

I had to find ways not to kill myself, so I whined in front of the chaplain, complained to the Internal Monitoring Board and ate a whole 900g pack of chocolate protein powder in one go.

A meeting with immigration had confirmed that I had to apply for immigration bail and that I would at least have to stay here for another ten days or so past my release date.

I had no choice but to arrange myself with the new situation, so after a few days I did. But I did not get my mojo back, I was just hanging around.

Then, just as it always had in the past, something entirely unexpected happened. I was called into the office by immigration.

An immigration officer stood in the office. It was the same one that had handed me the immigration bail application a week earlier. "Good news", he said.

"This is a warning letter".

He handed me the letter. It was from the home office.

'Careful consideration has been given to your conduct, your personal circumstances and the question of your liability to deportation. The representation submitted has also been considered. In light of the evidence available, it has been decided not to deport you from the United Kingdom (UK) on this occasion.'

"You will be released on Monday. But be careful, this is a warning letter. If you commit another offence, you will be deported."

"These are the best news I've had in a long time." I said to him. "Not many people get this letter", he told me. "Good luck."

He seemed happy for me. I imagine it to be a difficult job. It can't always be pleasant to tell people they'll be kicked out of the country.

It was probably the greatest piece of paper I'd ever seen in my life. When I called Bill he told me I should frame it and hang it on the wall.

A Reversal of Fortune

I now had more of a spring in my step, which didn't make the last few days in prison easier. I told every officer about the great news. The excitement was moderate. One officer actually didn't believe me. "Out the door? Have they told you that?" It seems to be that most of the inmates at the Foreign National weren't as lucky as I was...

My last day in prison was strangely similar to my first day in prison. Not to misunderstand me, it was a vastly happier day, of course. But what was the same was this sense of surrealness, this sense of: *Is this really happening?*

Then I walked out the door.

And suddenly there I was, standing on a street somewhere outside the prison. I stood there for a minute, and then walked down the road towards the train station. None of it was followed by fanfares and fireworks as I had imagined all these years.

You're simply walking down a street.

During my time in prison I'd often say to people "prison is the easy bit. The hard part comes after release" because I thought this to be true. I understood the weeks and months after release might be very difficult. That the world out there isn't as rosy as one imagines being locked in a cell.

But whether I really grasped it deep down, and whether I really had the right mindset, the right humble attitude, is another question.

CHAPTER 6: THE LIES WE TELL OURSELVES – COPING STRATEGIES IN PRISON

Reframing as Coping Strategy

I wrote in my diary around the time I arrived at the Training Prison: *'I know this might sound insane, but the fact is that if I had the choice between being here or going back to my life in Wembley living in a box room and working in that shitty waffle shop, I'd rather be here.'*

On several occasions I told fellow inmates that if I were to be released unexpectedly now, I'd have to say no, "I'm staying in prison", as I hadn't achieved all the things I set out to do yet.

This was a coping strategy. I had to tell myself that I wanted to be in prison and that I had things to do there.

What I did was create a narrative for myself. The narrative went as follows: There were so many things that I always wanted to do in life, but never had the time to, because I needed to work and pay my rent. Now that I was in prison, I was finally able to do those things. I was finally able to learn languages and educate myself.

What this reframing allowed me was to have a positive mindset. Prison was not going to be wasted time, no, it was an opportunity.

It enabled me to protect my mental health and to stay hopeful, rather than falling into a hole of despair. I was also able to look forward to the future. By the time I'd be released, I'd be in a better position, because I would have learnt so much.

Whilst some of this reframing borders on self-delusion, there was a certain truth to it. There is a resource you have in abundance in prison, but that is scarce on the outside. That resource is time. You can use the sudden wealth of free time to your advantage. So many other inmates simply didn't realise this. They focused on the things they couldn't do in prison, rather than focusing on the opportunities that prison could offer them.

Whereas prison in general is a loss of freedom, when it comes to not having to pay your rent, it actually increases your freedom.

Yes, I might have been unable to leave my cell, but when it came to how I would spend my time inside that cell, I was completely free. This is why I was struggling so much in double cells. In a shared cell, that last bit of freedom was taken from me. Whenever I was in double cell, I just couldn't handle it. Would this have been the situation over the entire three years, I would have needed to completely change my outlook; otherwise I wouldn't have made it. Thankfully that wasn't the case.

When it comes to mental health strategies, the reality of a situation is less important than how we evaluate things. In any situation we can choose to see the glass as half-empty or as half-full. I was therefore engaging in a constructive coping strategy. My reframing still had enough grounding in reality, however, to allow me to process my offending and not to avoid taking responsibility. I did not want to mitigate my responsibility or pretend that I hadn't really messed up; I just wanted to spend my sentence the most productive way possible.

Less Adaptive Strategies

An example of someone who took this reframing a little too far, was someone I met someone at the Training prison, a muscular guy who worked out a lot.

He started off with the same good idea, but then took it way too far.

He boasted to me that he had already written more than 100 pages of his book entitled: 'I chose prison.' Now that's full-blown self-delusion. Nobody chooses prison.

This guy also told me that he had three kids on the outside. I couldn't have imagined them being impressed by his declaration that he chose prison. As delusional as his strategy might have been, however, it was his way of being able to make it through the day. And that's not an easy thing to do in prison. Everyone has their own ways and tics of dealing with it, whether they're conscious or not.

Many of the coping mechanisms I saw involved some form or another of self-delusion. At the Training Prison I met an older Dutch guy who at first seemed out of place in prison. He was very educated and polite. The story he told me was that he ran a private university in Holland with his wife and they had been looking to open a branch in London. A large drug exchange took place at the hotel that they were staying at and he received 25 years for drug dealing. He had simply been in the wrong place at the wrong time. It was simply too far-fetched. Nevertheless, you almost believed him because he was so convincing. Did he actually believe in his innocence?

Maybe he had to do so in order to cope? How else do you deal with a 25-year sentence? Or maybe he was done for an altogether different offence that he didn't want to admit? The important thing to take away is to always take what other inmates tell you with a teaspoon of Hollandaise.

The Coping Strategies of my Various Cellmates

What was telling in Brendan's reframing of the realities of the works is that all his offences were in England. If anything, in his mind, he did the right thing. Going to prison was a worthy price to pay for taking the moral high ground. If there is anyone to blame, it's the bastards who run that cesspit, shithole country of Europe.

Z was still in full denial mode and hadn't come to terms with what happened. He still hadn't faced up to the reality of the situation and therefore didn't make any plans for his time in prison. The fact that he was in remand limbo did not help him a bit with this. His obsessive cleanliness on the other hand was an unconscious way for him to be able to pretend that he still had some control over his situation.

As for Jason, in the long term, smashing up the prison cell was obviously a maladaptive strategy, and led to many problems, such as having debts with the prison service. In the moment, however, it did actually help him. Once he had the pent-up anger out of him, he was calmer. He just needed to get it out of him. His problem was that that was all he had in his mental arsenal and that he had never learnt a different, more adaptive coping strategy.

Jason's family had some connections to big shots in the crime world, going back all the way to the Krays. He told me this with gleaming pride, and planned to write a book about his family story, his life of crime and his incarceration.

Writing a book in prison has become a cliché, but one can see how it can be a cathartic experience. Apart from that, there also needs to be the hope, maybe even secret dream that your dreadful situation will change completely one day. You'll write a book about it all and make it big. Even if that stays a secret, ridiculous dream, it might be something you need for yourself, to keep you going.

Vlad on the other hand was the pragmatic, productive type. He was running his vodka business and distillery. On several occasions the tried to recruit me, explaining that I should make myself busy and useful. To him, my attempts to study and read were a complete waste of time, it was he who was the one spending his time productively. That is, when he wasn't off his face, which is how he spent all his time when he wasn't 'working.'

Then there was the strategy of my only cellmate at the Training Prison, the Spice head, which is a very common strategy. The more miserable the conditions in any prison, the more common this strategy becomes. Numbing yourself by being high on Spice all day.

I remember a conversation I had with a nurse at the Foreign National. We were talking about Spice, and she was telling me how dangerous Spice was and how important it was to stay healthy in prison. I almost wanted to scream at her:"Do you not see the contradiction? Look around. You're talking about the importance of staying healthy yet you throw us into this horrible dump and don't even feed us enough to get by." As always, I kept my opinion to myself. She seemed convinced that prisoners take Spice because they feel guilty of their crime. In reality, prisoners take Spice because the conditions are so dreadful.

The way how Tinto – my cellmate at the Foreign National – dealt with it all was both impressive but also annoying. "My patience is my superpower" is what he used to say. And it was true.

He had all the patience in the world and nothing would affect him. He wasn't stupid, but he'd just switch off his brain, leave it in the corner and watch stupid sitcoms all day. Every now and then laughing like an idiot. If he saw the same commercial for the 1000th time that same day, it wouldn't affect him a bit (whereas I'd fly through the roof with rage).

It was admirable and impressive, but what infuriated me about him was the complete lack of ambition. He did not mind one bit that he completely wasted his time and did nothing.

Prison is Not Equal

This is a very important point to mention. I was able to make prison work for me because I had access to resources. I had a certain level of education. And I was extremely lucky that I had family who was able and willing to financially support me while I was in prison. Many don't have this. The fact is that how much rehabilitation in British prisons is possible depends on how much support a prisoner has from the outside. A prisoner needs money to supplement the inadequate diet. A prisoner needs money for learning materials.

The terrible irony of imprisonment in the UK is that the prisoners who can actually benefit from it, rehabilitate and turn their lives around, are the ones who need the help the least in the first place.

The prisoners who really need the help are let down completely by the system. It's the 'inverse care law' in action. The areas of the UK that are the most deprived and need resources the most do actually get the fewest. Whereas richer areas that already have the most resources in the first place, such as London, get the most.

Making it Through the Day With a Solid Structure

The most important thing in prison is to have a structure. You need to know why you're there and you need to have a routine of how you're going to spend the day that feels like you're achieving something.

I remember running in the pouring rain one day when someone told me that I was crazy to run in this weather. My reply was: "So what if it rains ten days in a row? Does that mean I won't go running for ten days?" It's all about the routine. If you keep a routine that is independent of what happens around you, you're able to stay sane and strong. If you make yourself dependent on the prison regime, you get thrown around like a rag doll.

Prisoners who manage their sentence well have a routine that gives them a sense of purpose. The ones that do less well, on the other hand, often have only one goal: to do their time. This doesn't work. It's simply not enough of a goal, especially if you have years to go. Time in prison is long. Without a structure and a purpose, just a single day can last an eternity. You need to find something inside prison that gives you purpose. And you need to have a solid, structured routine.

Writing Therapy

Writing can be a really powerful tool in processing emotions. My diary helped me enormously in making it through the day, coming to terms with what was happening and trying to give my prison existence meaning.

Whenever things become really difficult, writing down my frustrations helped me not to despair. When I was trapped in a tiny cell and my cellmate was driving me crazy, writing somehow helped me to release all the frustration and the pent-up anger. When it was really bad and it become impossible to meditate because I was so agitated, I could always still write. Writing saved my life on several occasions.

Exercise, Meditation, Things to Look Forward to

Daily exercise is essential. It makes you feel better physically as well as mentally. The important thing is to have an exercise routine that you can do in your cell. Do not make yourself dependent on being able to go to the gym or the exercise yard. It will lead to frustrations. Gym and exercise often get cancelled; do not depend on them for your wellbeing. In addition, the three gym slots a week simply aren't enough.

Meditation follows the same principle of not being dependent on what happens in the prison. You can meditate anytime. An overwhelming amount of research shows that meditation improves mental health.[1] It helps you to control your thoughts and emotions. Over time, you learn to calm the 'monkey brain'. The Phoenix trust is a fantastic charity that sends out free meditation and yoga booklets to prisoners. [2]

Apart from a solid routine, it is crucial to have things to look forward to. For me this was the daily newspaper, the radio, my books.

Confronting your Demons

How much the other inmates confronted their offending is difficult for me to say as I wasn't there when they attended programs, spoke to their offender manager or psychologist.

Some did not want to talk about their crimes, but many were very open about them. What I did notice is that very often, they couldn't explain their offending themselves. I often heard things such as "and then it happened" or "and then it came over me". I do not want to suggest that they didn't assume responsibility; more often than not they were simply as mystified as the next person why they had done it.

Which is a problem because I think it is very important to be able to make sense of it all. A prisoner needs to go through his sentence creating a coherent story of why he offended, how he has grown and changed since then, and why he won't offend again. This coherent story provides a narrative that can lead to a better future. There was a reason why you had to be in prison. You had to learn certain things and make amends. But now that chapter is finished and the next chapter where you are able to rebuild your life starts. I don't see how any prisoners can heal and do his sentence successfully without a narrative that at least provides some clarity and closure.

When it comes to my own offending, I have sought to understand why I did it and created a narrative that explains things and makes sure it won't happen again.

In the years leading up to my offence, things looked ok from the outside. But the truth is that I was struggling constantly. Apart from doing my job well, I managed nothing in life. It was a disaster. Rather than making friends and trying to find a relationship, I sat at home in my box room every weekend doing coke. Despite earning good money I did not manage to save penny; instead I spent £25k on parking tickets.

I was living life like a zombie because I carried a trauma with me that hadn't been addressed. I had psychological injuries stemming from my childhood that I never successfully managed to heal. A lot of things quite simply went wrong when I was a small child and when I grew up, and they weren't addressed when they should have been addressed – during my time as teenager and in my early 20s. Instead, because of family dynamics and my own inability to understand what was wrong, they were reinforced over the next decades. Whenever things seemed looked more or less ok from the outside, like when I had decent jobs, it enabled me to fail to recognise that there was something deeply wrong.

What changed was that my time in prison has forced me to confront these issues. In addition, family dynamics have changed with family members dying and my parents becoming older. This has opened a window to change things for the first time and provide clarity, closure and healing. A year of therapy since my release has helped with it, too.

If I could give one advice to any young person today is that when there is something wrong, it's important not to sweep it under the carpet, as difficult as that may be. Mental health is incredibly important. It is the foundation of everything. I've ruined 20 years of my life because I didn't properly address my issues. For parents, my advice would be not to hope that issues will resolve themselves automatically, because they won't. Resolving your mental health issues is the foundation for everything else.

That's the psychological explanation in short form. It tries to explain things and maybe it lets me off the hook a little.

The simpler explanation would be that I was stupid and I fucked up. Maybe it's as simple as that and there's not much more to it. I simply fucked up and made a massive mistake.

CHAPTER 7: PUBLIC OPINION, POLITICS & THE MEDIA

The public hold contradictory views when it comes to crime and prison.

People clearly want rehabilitation and don't believe that sending more people to prison is effective in dealing with crime. In a survey of 2018, only 7% of respondents thought that having more people in prison was effective in reducing crime, whilst 33% wanted more rehabilitation for those in prison.[1]

In a study by the Centre for Crime and Justice Studies, only 8% said that sending more people to prison was effective in reducing crime, whilst 53% thought that most people come out of prison worse than when they went in.[2]

These are encouraging numbers that show that the public understands that more people in prison isn't the solution and that rehabilitation is important.

What is interesting then is that more than 65% of the public think that sentences aren't harsh enough and should be longer.[3]

This is exactly what I explained in the introduction: People want rehabilitation, but they also want harsher punishment; which is of course a contradiction.

Furthermore, the public are misinformed when it comes to crime and sentencing. In a 2022 survey, only 2% of the public were aware that crime had been falling and that overall crime rates today are lower than they were in the 1990s, with the majority thinking that crime is on the rise.[4] Equally, only 2% were aware that average sentence had increased massively over the last 25 years, with the majority falsely thinking sentences are getting more lenient.[5]

A misinformed public put politicians in a difficult situation. Is it worth the risk of trying to shape public opinion? If a politician proposes anything progressive, they risk not only the ire of the public, but also that of the right of their party and face a lynching by the tabloid press. It's simply not worth the risk.

Prison reform is a quagmire that no politician wants to get into. It presents nothing but trouble. Sooner or later, you'll be accused of rewarding criminals whilst punishing hardworking, decent families and victims of crime.

The only thing politicians are never afraid to say is that they are 'tough on crime'. Because what's not to like? Who wouldn't want to be tough on crime and the consequences of crime?

The problem with being 'tough on crime' is that when prisons are overcrowded and crumbling you are actually being very soft on crime. Government policy of overfilling prisons without funding them properly has had disastrous consequences. It has ensured that criminality is rife inside prisons and that many reoffend when they leave prison.[6] It has also ensured that drug use is rampant behind bars and that some who have never had substance become addicts inside.[7] It has led to an increase in mental health problems amongst prisoners,[8] leading to additional problems after release and the possibility of reoffending. At the same time, it has made the working environment for officers and others who work in prisons a dangerous nightmare.[9] All of these are consequences of being 'tough on crime'.

The biggest problem of how crime and prison is often represented is that there is this false dichotomy.

You are either on the side of the victims of crime, or you're on the side of the criminals. There's no in-between, no explanation that things are a bit more complicated than that.

If you're 'tough on crime', handing down ever harsher sentences, you are on the side of the victims. If you call for prison reform, on the other hand, you side with criminals.

Anyone who is over the age of 11 should understand that this sort of thinking is stupid and has nothing to do with the complex realities of society. But this is exactly how the public conversation has been held in this country for the last few decades, and hardly anyone dares to try to explain the issues in a manner that is a bit more nuanced.

Another problem is our constant exposure to the media. Almost on a daily basis we read and hear about the most terrible examples of cruel and heinous crimes committed. These crimes do happen of course and the consequences for the victims are horrible and all too real. But because the most shocking crimes always make headline news, they distort our perception.[10] We read about a serial killer and think that's what most criminals and most people in prison are like. We might not do so consciously, but are nevertheless influenced by what we hear and see.

Sometime when I listen to the news on the radio or read the newspaper I wonder whether it is really necessary to report on every instance of crime committed. Is it really in the national interest to report about any stabbing in any small town? It is very significant for the local police and for everyone involved, but does the entire nation need to hear about it? Wouldn't it be better to every once in a while put the sensational news in relation with the actual overall numbers of crime (And without distorting those numbers!).

The interplay of media, public opinion and politics has created a self-reinforcing triangle leading us to the situation today. The public is misinformed through media exposure. Politicians make decisions that reinforce wrong perceptions rather than challenging them. It is a self-reinforcing cycle that is hard to break.

But it is a cycle that is malleable. Every time one part of the triangle gives way a little, the other parts have the opportunity to make a step in the right direction. Over time, with the change of attitudes in society, the cycle can be broken.

When it comes to the public, this is not an easy ask. Especially for those who have experienced the terrible consequences of crime first hand. But a change in attitude does not have to come from sympathy with offenders. It can simply come from knowing the facts and that the current system achieves the opposite of what it claims to do. Being 'soft on crime' in reality actually means pursuing policies that reduce further crime. Being 'soft on crime' therefore actually means being tough on crime.

The media have to think about their part in shaping public opinion and playing a part in creating the kind of society we live in. Aren't there better ways to do this than always showing the worst of humanity and portraying it in the most terrible light possible?

Rather than adapting their views to what they think the public want to hear, politicians should follow their convictions and convince the public with passion. This country has a huge problem with distrust of politicians, who are basically all considered liars.[11] The fact that politicians flip-flop on their views based on what they believe will win them votes plays a huge part in this. More honest politicians who act with conviction will also increase public trust in politics.

The current prison crisis has opened a window for the status quo to be changed. The public is now more receptive to new ideas, as it has become obvious that the current system isn't working.

There are two possible directions to take.

The first is to continue as before and build as many prison places as quickly as possible.

The second is to change things and reform the system.

As the first option has actually become impossible to achieve, the government seems to be pursuing a mix of 1 and 2. Build more places, but also reform (without going too far).[12]

How the next years will pan out will, in my opinion, depend on how much the government will dare to move from the status quo towards reform. And it will of course depend on what the governments that follow will do.

I do not think I have to point this out, but I'll do it anyway because it is important: prison reformers don't do what they do because they want to reward crime and punish victims. Even just writing this makes it clear how absurd it is. Prison reformers know what is going wrong and want to improve the system because it will benefit everyone. Most importantly, it will benefit the victims of crime.

CHAPTER 8: THE VICTIMS OF CRIME

I listened to the French podcast 'Legend' whilst being at the gym when I heard this story that really affected me. I listened to it twice and later downloaded the audiobook.[1]

'Le magicien a failli disparaître – the magician who almost disappeared'.

Alexandre Bernard tells the story of how he almost lost his life to a drunk driver.

He was hired to stage a magic show outside of Paris. After staying at a hotel, he was on the road the next morning, when a car coming from the opposite direction crashed into him full-frontal at 140 km/h.

Bernard was kept alive by a bystander who talked to him for 2 hours until the emergency services were finally able to cut him out of the wreck. He was hardly able to talk, as his jaw had been shattered and all of his teeth were loose at the back of his throat.

At the nearest hospital, he was immediately told that his case was too severe for them to handle and he was sent via helicopter to a specialist unit, at which point he was sure he was going to die. He couldn't feel or move his legs.

He had a broken thigh bone, broken arm, broken ankles, a broken sacrum and his jaw was basically pulverised – his face was completely disfigured. After the operation that reconstructed his face, his jaw was put together with metal bars, meaning he couldn't open his mouth.

Because of the unbearable pain he was given the highest dose of morphine. This led him to constantly having to throw up through his nose.

For 42 days he was not able to get up from his hospital bed. There was a very high chance he wasn't ever going to be able to walk again.

After a few months however, he did manage to move his leg slightly. He was given a wheelchair and now had to learn to walk again from scratch.

For the next few months he would spend hours every day in rehabilitation, painstakingly learning to walk again. All in all, it took him about 8 years to fully recover.

Today, he can walk with a very slight limp but if he needs to cover longer distances – like going to a theme park with his daughter – he needs to bring the wheelchair, which he still has in his car.

The driver of the other vehicle was a 25-year-old who showed no remorse. When asked by his lawyer of whether to sue, Bernard at first said no, and that it was "a youngster and mistakes can happen". He changed his mind after a friend told him about a facebook post in which the 25-year had written: "a little accident won't keep me from drinking again". He did also not apologise or attempt to contact Bernard.

The sentence the drunk-driver received was a suspended prison sentence of one year, plus suspension of his driving license, which Bernard complains is much too lenient.

But what was the worst for him was the lack of remorse. Had the 25-year-old called him and apologised, Bernard says, he would have forgiven him, because "mistakes can happen".

Bernard tells his story because he wants to warn others of the dangers of drunk driving. "Don't ever drive drunk. Jamais. Never".

The question I have to ask myself is this: Would I see things differently had I been on the other side? What if someone in my family had been killed by a drunk driver? How would I feel about that driver? What if I'd found the love of my life and our future together would have been ended by a drunk driver, would I consider three years imprisonment a fair sentence? Or, what if I would find myself in a wheelchair for the rest of my life because of a drunk driver? Would I care about the conditions in prison? Would I write a book calling for prison reform? Or would I instead wish the perpetrator would rot in hell.

These aren't pleasant things to think about, but they are the reality for victims of crime.

I try to view things from the other side, to put myself in the shoes of those that I have harmed, and those that others like me have harmed. That is, at least as far as that's possible, because in reality you can never know how you will feel about a given situation, unless you actually find yourself in that situation.

We are very much trained to be partisan, something which our adversarial court system reinforces. It's simply difficult to see things from the other side's perspective because we hardly ever do it. In public discourse on crime, for example, the conversation is always framed from the victim's perspective, because nobody imagines they could end up being the perpetrator.

When I was at the Training Prison I spoke to an officer about my crime and my sentence. He told me that he thought 3 years imprisonment was too little for what I had done. He added that if a drunk driver had killed his daughter, he would want the driver to be behind bars for at least 30 years.

What struck me is that he did not consider the possibility that his daughter could actually be the drunk driver and not the victim. Had his daughter made the decision to drive after having had a few drinks, causing a fatal accident, would he then also want her behind bars for at least 30 years?

We never consider the possibility that we could end up being the perpetrator. But the fact is that perpetrators are just as human as victims.

During my first time at the Foreign National, I received the terrible news from my mom that our family friend Heinz had died. He was a dentist who had just sold his practice to enjoy his retirement. Apart from horses, a boat, and a fast motorcycle, he also had a tendency to pack way too many things into one day. Riding too fast on his bike, he was hit by a car coming from the other direction that turned left into a driveway and didn't see him. He was fast enough that he was probably dead on the spot. The driver of the other vehicle was an 80-year old who simply didn't see him coming from the other direction as he turned left.

The way Heinz's family handled it was extremely mature. There was of course a lot of sadness, but complete acceptance and no anger or blame towards the driver of the other vehicle. There could have easily been angry lamentations such as "wasn't he too old to drive at 80? He should have still seen him, from a certain age people shouldn't be allowed to drive", but there weren't, because Heinz's family understood that this approach isn't productive.

When Victims Make Laws

Imagine it had been found out that the 80-year old driver had been drinking. Looking at it from one angle, it would have changed absolutely nothing. Looking at it from a different one, it would have changed everything. An accident was now a crime. An old driver that had our sympathy was now possibly the target of our anger.

It would have allowed Heinz's family to channel their grief into anger and hatred towards the person that was clearly at fault.

A different, but more productive way in which victims channel their grief is by campaigning to change legislation, especially if they feel the judicial outcome in their case was unjust.

They get in contact with their MP, who then – often successfully – proposes to change legislation in parliament.

This often creates laws that are less fair than they were before, because the law for everyone has been changed based on a single case.

If the maximum penalty for a certain crime is increased, for example, it means that all sentences for this crime across the board will be harsher. This is one of the reasons for the sentence inflation we have seen in the last few decades.

If your family member is the victim of a knife crime, it's an instinctual reaction to call for harsher sentences for knife crimes. But when knife crimes are already punished harshly, it will have little effect to increase sentences further, other than sending offenders to prison for too long. It will also have the negative effect of distracting from the need to address the root causes of knife crime which are societal. "We've increased the sentence, job done."

As a result, knife crime will increase further while prisons become ever more overcrowded and dysfunctional.

What is Justice?

Did my prison sentence of three years represent justice? Of course not. In the strictest sense of its meaning, justice would have meant for me to die.

But that wouldn't have necessarily been justice, either.

The fact is that I have committed an act of irreversible injustice. The injustice that I have caused cannot be remedied, regardless of how much time I spend in prison, how much I have to suffer myself or how much remorse I have.

I am acutely aware that if you measure amount of suffering, three years in prison is comparatively little. But isn't me being able to try to redeem myself a little and trying to do something productive, positive with my life better than endless years in prison?

I am constantly struggling with the question if I have the right to say anything at all. That talk about crime and its victims coming from me is hypocritical and tactless. The biggest worry for me in writing this book was that I was neglecting the terrible experience of victims and failing to see the victims' point of view. Or that I would in some way cause additional injury by seeming to be disrespectful. It is such a sensitive topic.

But ultimately I believe that an honest, open conversation is important. It's important that I try to process what I did. Writing gives me meaning. It gives me a future that makes sense. Isn't that more positive than forever living in the shadow of what happened?

Writing this book is my way of processing; just as for many victims trying to improve laws and society to prevent further victims is their way of processing it, their way of trying to turn it into something positive. Whether you're the victim or the perpetrator, you need to come to terms with what happened. If you're the perpetrator it's especially important, because you need to learn from it and change.

CHAPTER 9 : WHAT WOULD A BETTER PRISON SYSTEM LOOK LIKE?

One of the most striking things about prison is that it is such a strange and barbaric institution, yet we see it as completely natural and inevitable. Most of us couldn't imagine a society without prisons, and advocates of prison abolition are considered lunatics that live in a fantasy world.

I remember a fellow inmate telling me:"Well, there have always been prisons and there will always be prisons."

But that isn't true at all. The prisons we know today are a relatively new invention from the 18th and 19th century.[1] Before that, prisons existed – one famous example being the Tower of London – but they mostly held a few debtors and political prisoners. Prison as punishment didn't exist; what was used instead was corporal punishment, public ridicule, banishment, transportation to penal colonies, and public executions.[2] When executions fell out of favour with the public and control of the American colonies was lost, prisons were built to fill the gap.

The prison that existed in the 19th century is fundamentally the same as that of today; we even still use some of the same buildings. That is the case despite the fact that our knowledge of human psychology, of biology, criminology and society has changed completely since then. We live in a different world, yet our prisons are the same.

I admit that just because an institution hasn't changed much, it does not necessarily follow that it is out of place in the world of today – Universities haven't fundamentally changed either since the 19th century. But prison is one of those institutions nobody questions just because it exists. Prisons are taken for granted and no alternative can be imagined. In addition, most people would rather not think about prison, which is understandable.

It's only when you've lived inside prisons that you realise what odd places they really are. I've had this moment many times when I walked through the wing and thought: *This place is so weird.*

Isn't it such a strange thing to create giant human warehouses and lock thousands in tiny cells? We mostly aren't talking about people that are so dangerous that they have to be securely locked away. We are talking about nearly 90,000 people, for the majority of whom that level of security is simply over the top. The US is much worse, with nearly 2 million people in prison.[3] That is the population of a small country – it is utterly insane.

Are we really saying that nearly two million people are so dangerous and evil that they have to be warehoused in this barbaric manner?

There is broad agreement that the UK prison system is flawed at best, broken at worst. Through my own experience I have shown you how this plays out in the daily life of prisoners. I would go further and question the entire institution of prison in its current form.

What I'm not advocating, however, is to close all prisons tomorrow and set everyone free. That would be a complete disaster. With all its flaws, prison does serve certain purposes that we need it for.

We read about terrible crimes in the media almost every day, and these crimes do happen and there need to be consequences for the people who commit them. There also needs to be safety for the victims in danger. Criminal justice is needed as glue to hold society together. Sure, most people wouldn't rob a bank even if it were allowed; but a few more people might, therefore a deterrent is needed. And there are some really nasty, nasty people that need to be locked away for public safety. If someone is planning a terrorist attack to kill thousands for example, of course they need to be locked away.

So How Do We Square This?

How can we create a prison system that still fulfils its function of public protection, punishment and deterrence, but also functions to rehabilitate and thereby cut future crime; all while costing less?

I believe it is completely possible in theory, but in practice has been impossible so far due to the interplay of politics, the media and public opinion I have explained earlier.

I need to stress that I am not a professional expert in penology or criminology. Equally, I do not have the experience of those that are working in the prison system. A prison governor might well read this and say to himself: "If it were only this easy. I think he's a bit naive." Officers who have to deal with the most difficult and dangerous individuals on a daily basis might equally question some of my views. I do not claim to always be 100% correct or have all the answers. I am just someone who has spent a few years in prison and shown an interest in the system. But that might give me a unique angle. I might see some truths that are hidden from officers and governors who are restricted on seeing things from the other end.

What I want to do is to start a conversation, to propose ideas. And that's really important, because:

1. The current system isn't working

2. There is still no open conversation about what needs to change

The discourse is still almost entirely focused on, "we're in crisis because we haven't built enough prisons", and "we need to build more prisons"; completely ignoring the core issue.

This seems to change now a little bit with the review of sentencing led by David Gaucke that might well lead to some changes very similar to what I will propose on the following pages.[4]

As I've said, we cannot just close all prisons. Nor can we create a completely new system from the ground up in the next few years. Change needs to be gradual.

I've therefore divided this chapter into three sections, following this gradual change.

The first describes changes that can be made under the current system. Prison charities such as the Howard League have been proposing some of them for years and many are in consideration to be implemented under the sentencing review led by David Gaucke as mentioned above. They would improve the situation.

However, they don't address the fundamentals of why prison doesn't work, in my opinion. I am questioning the entire institution of prison in its current form and there's no question that prison in the future will look very different.

What is also not addressed is that prison is entwined with society. Crime is a societal issue that criminal justice alone cannot solve. For a better prison system with fewer inmates and better outcomes, changes in society have to be made.

The second part is therefore centred at what needs to happen in society through government action. What kind of society breeds crime? What role does the futile war against drugs have to play?

Only once changes in society have been made can we have a different prison system.

The third part focuses on my (slightly utopian) vision of prison in the future. I am aware that this complete re-structuring of prison from the ground up is not a practical solution at the moment and has to come gradually. The changes would have to be introduced over many years, after the smaller changes introduced in part 1 and 2 have been implemented. Considering constantly changing governments with different agendas and priorities, this is not an easy task.

IMPROVEMENTS UNDER THE CURRENT SYSTEM

In summary, they mean 'less prison' and more use of alternative forms of criminal justice. Even the current prison minister James Timpson has suggested that only a third of prisoners belong in prison.[5] In my opinion, prison should be reserved for dangerous individuals who pose an immediate physical or psychological risk to others. Too many people are in prison because of mental health issues, addiction problems, and poverty. They simply shouldn't be in prison, but receive the help they need in the community, together with types of punishments available in the community, if needed.

But I also think that there are some offences for which more people should be in prison. These include rape, domestic violence, coercive control. Less than 1 out of 100 rapists actually gets convicted.[6] Coercive control and domestic violence paint a similar picture for many complicated reasons, such as victims not coming forward due to the nature of coercion. As a result of the massive court backlog, many rape victims simply give up.[7] More violent and sexual crimes need to be solved and more offenders successfully prosecuted.

More resources should be invested to deal with these types of offences and fewer for chasing those who grow a few herbal plants in their attic.

Restrict Use of Remand to Those Who Pose Immediate Danger to Others

Too many are held on remand for too long – often for many months and even years. The number of 17,000 unsentenced prisoners is the highest it has ever been and a main contributor to the crisis of overcrowding.[8] Many of those held on remand will not actually receive a custodial sentence, meaning they should have never been in prison in the first place.[9] The presumption of innocence that forms the basis of our understanding of just law is completely disregarded when people are locked up without having been convicted.

Someone should only be detained on remand when they pose an immediate danger, either physically or psychologically, to others. In this case they need to be held on remand to protect others. In all other cases, bail should be given. Strict bail conditions can mitigate the risk of flight and other concerns.

Restricting remand to those posing an immediate threat to others would not just ease overcrowding but lead to a criminal justice system that is fairer, with fewer innocent people in prison.

Make Recall Requirements Stricter

Just as with remand, the recall prisoner population of 12,000 is the highest it has ever been, contributing to overcrowding.[10] Too many are recalled. And the vast majority of recalls are not for further offences, but for non-compliance.[11] Often prisoners are recalled only based on suspicion. If a prisoner is recalled incorrectly, they often have to stay in prison for months before the parole board is able to review the decision and revoke it.[12] This was the case with Lenny, whom you might remember from the transport to the Training Prison. He was one of the two adults behaving like children. Lenny was recalled because his ex-wife had called probation, as she was angry with him for whatever reason. He hadn't actually done anything wrong, which was eventually confirmed in the investigation. He was released, but only after having been imprisoned for nearly six months. Six extra months of prison for a wrong allegation is a bitter pill to swallow.

The conditions for recall should be made stricter without compromising safety. One way to do this would be to return the power to recall to the courts. That would mean that there would be more robust processes in place, and fewer would be recalled unnecessarily.

Expand Use of Community Orders

Community orders are a lot cheaper than prison sentences.[13] They are also less disruptive and have better outcomes in terms of reoffending. Much more use should be made of community orders, especially in regard to issues such as petty crime in connection with substance abuse issues. Many of these could be tailored to the offender and the type of offence.

Home Detention Curfews (house arrest) are a form of punishment but they would allow the offender to stay in employment and not become homeless, both of which are risk factors for further crime.

Introduce ICROs (Intense Control and Rehabilitation Orders)

These are a form of community order proposed as an alternative to prison sentences of up to three years. Offenders are kept on house arrest and their whereabouts are monitored through GPS tagging.

They are ordered to receive education, training, rehabilitative support as well as addiction and mental health treatment as required in the community, where these services are much better than in prison.

This type of sentence could replace most of shorter prison sentences under 3 years. They would be much more cost effective and have better rehabilitative outcomes.

Expand Out-of-Court Solutions

Many more offences could be resolved out of court.[14] Courts are massively overburdened, and this would relieve the pressure. Magistrates often hand fines that offenders aren't able to pay in any case.

The police already make use of out-of-court settlements. For example, a shoplifter might be referred to addiction services and repay the damage caused, rather than having to appear in court.

These should be expanded and used more often, in order to take pressure off the courts and have better outcomes in reducing offending.

This could also be a process in which the victims are more involved. Through dialogue with the offender, they could have more of an input what sort of compensation would constitute a restoration of justice.

More Funding For Mental Health and Addiction Support in the Community

For small crimes to be settled out of court, the support needs to be there in the community to divert offenders to addiction programs and mental health support. The addiction programs that already exist have excellent outcomes, but there aren't enough of them.[15]

Austerity after the financial crash of 2008 has had a negative impact on crime through the financial starvation of community services. These services need to be revived and even more needs to be invested. The money spent will be compensated for by ultimately having to spend less on prison.

Reduce the Use of Short Prison Sentences of Under 12 Months

Short sentences often do more harm than good. They offer no rehabilitation and have worse reoffending outcomes than community orders.[16]

Whilst not completely abolishing short sentences as they might be the only option in certain cases, the presumption should be to avoid them and give a community order instead.

Sentence Reform: The Length Handed in Court Should Reflect the Actual Prison Time Served

It is very confusing for victims that the sentence length does not actually reflect the time spent in prison. What usually happens in case of a determinate sentence is that offenders spend half of their sentence in prison, the other half in the community on license. For more some specific type of violent sentences, offenders now have to spend two-thirds of their sentence in prison.

There should be a sentencing reform to end this confusing system. The sentence handed in court should be the actual time spent in prison. In my case, therefore, the sentence would have been 3 years imprisonment.

This would also create the opportunity to set the length of the license period based on each individual case. These would relieve the pressure for probation as it would reduce the number of people under supervision in the community. In many cases, it's simply not necessary to supervise offenders for many years after release.

This sentence reform would also provide the opportunity to look at sentence lengths across the board and reduce them in the most extreme cases where sentence have become disproportionately long.

Release all IPP Prisoners That are Over Tariff

The IPP (Imprisonment for Public Protection) sentence was introduced by the Labour government in 2003. It is essentially a 99-year sentence given to repeat offenders with two or more convictions of a violent nature, even if minor. Instead of receiving a sentence of fixed length, IPP prisoners receive a tariff and can only be released when the parole board decides that it is safe to do so.

The problem was that IPPs were often given for quite minor offences, that way too many were given, and that it was impossible for offenders to prove that it was safe to release them, often because they couldn't access the courses necessary. Many therefore stayed in prison forever, despite short tariffs for minor crimes.

The IPP sentence was abolished in 2012, but not for those already convicted. Today there are still nearly 3,000 IPP prisoners still in prison, all of them many years over tariff.[17] They are victims of a deeply unjust law and should be released.

Send Prisoners to Correct Institution Directly from Court

There is simply too much moving around of prisoners that are low and medium risk. Why isn't it possible to send everyone to the correct institution straight from court? Instead, everyone is crammed into a local prison, just to be moved on shortly after. It's unnecessary and inefficient. Security categorisation could take place at the point of sentencing in most cases.

In my case, I could have easily been sent straight to the Training Prison (category C, which was my initial security category) from court. Many low-risk offenders could be sent to open prisons straight from court – or at least to a training prison – rather than having to go to the local hellhole.

Improve the Food in Prison: Not just Through More Money but Through a Change in Culture and Attitude

This seems a point of minor importance, but I actually believe that improving the food in prison could have ripple effect that would improve things in many other areas.

The comparative costs would be comparatively low – increasing the food budget to £5 for every prisoner would cost less than £80 million a year. Of course that's a lot of money, but considering that reoffending costs more than £18 billion a year, it shows how much it could actually save in the long run.

To me it's clear that the only way to improve the system is to improve it from the ground up. Unless the food in prison improves, there's little hope that the rest will improve, either.

Dial Down the Politicising of Criminal Justice

Imagine your toddler gets attacked by a man with a machete. In order to defend the life of your child, you punch the man. Afterwards, you find yourself in court, charged with assault. When you try to explain the reasons for attacking the man, the court explains that you are not permitted to state the context in which you committed your offence. In other words: the only thing that counts is that you punched the man; evidence showing he threatened your child with an axe is not permissible.

This is exactly what's happening in UK courts today. Climate protesters are not allowed to talk about the climate crisis and resulting existential threat for humanity in court.[18]

A Just Stop Oil activist was handed 20 months imprisonment for throwing a can of tomato soup at a painting by Van Gogh, which was protected by glass and therefore not damaged.[19] Nearly 2 years of prison is a ridiculous sentence for staging a peaceful protest by throwing a can of soup. Had the motive been anarchy and not the climate, the result would have been a fine and no prison.

What's happening here is a clear erosion of democracy. The right to protest and the right to free speech have been curtailed. The UK cracks down harder on climate protesters than any other country in the world.[20]

Of course it shouldn't be acceptable for protestors to use climate change as an excuse to do whatever they like. Criminal damage still is criminal damage. Also, there need to be limits to how disruptive protest can be and there need to be consequences when people go too far. But the right to protest in the UK has been stifled to a degree where it has simply gone too far.

Prisoners Should be Given the Right to Vote

"It makes me physically ill to even contemplate having to give the vote to anyone who is in prison" (David Cameron, Prime Ministers Question's in the House of Commons, Nov. 2010)[21]

A lot can happen in 15 years and I'd like to think that attitudes since then have changed. The right to vote is a basic human right. People that are sent to prison lose their liberty, but not their citizenship or their basic human rights. In a democratic society, every citizen has the right to vote without any stipulations. An asshole has the same right to vote as a Samaritan. That is the point of democracy. Not giving the right to vote to prisoners is therefore undemocratic.

In addition, giving prisoners the vote could change public attitudes. It would make it clearer that prisoners are human beings and still form part of society. For prisoners, it would give them a sense that they aren't cast away for good and can still have a stake in society if they participate.

SOCIETAL CHANGES

An important feature of the 'tough on crime' approach has been to peddle the myth that crime can be addressed by sending more people to prison for longer. This has disastrous consequences, as it diverts attention away from addressing the root causes of crime in society. Humans are the same everywhere in the world, yet crime rates differ vastly. We need to examine what causes crime in society and use countries with lower crime rates as examples to follow.

More Equality

Societies that are more equal have lower crime rates.

The Equality Trust writes: 'The link between inequality and homicide rates has been shown in as many as 40 studies, and the differences are large: there are five-fold differences in murder rates between countries related to inequality. The most important reason why violence is more common in unequal societies is that it is often triggered by people feeling looked down, disrespected and loss of face. We have also found that inequality is related to the Global Peace Index and violence against children.' [22]

Whilst the UK is more equal than the US and has lower crime rates; in the international comparison of developed countries it fares very badly on both.

In the international comparison on crime rates it ranks at 57, i.e. crime in the UK is comparatively high.[23] At the same time, it ranks 46th in inequality, i.e. the UK is a very unequal society.[24] The 10 countries with the lowest crime rates in the world are all significantly more equal than the UK. This shows the potential of reducing crime in the UK by increasing equality.

What's interesting is that a pilot project on Universal Basic Income showed that those given a universal basic income were less likely to commit crimes.[25]

Equally, homelessness is associated with crime. It is known, for example, that a homeless prison leaver is twice as likely to reoffend.[26] Reducing homelessness would therefore also be helpful in reducing crime rates.

Legalisation of Drugs

Drug prohibition is a major driver of criminality. In many ways, the failed war on drugs and the failing prison system are two sides of the same coin. Behind both of them is the same flawed ideology.

The idea of the war on drugs is that you can use sheer force, ceaseless enforcement and strictest punishment to force the illegal drug trade into submission. Following its own logic, all that needs to be done is to lock up all drug dealers and the problem is solved. We need to bombard normal human behaviour into submission until there are no drugs left. If that doesn't work, we just need to use more force and more violence.

The war on drugs has been a failure of epic proportions. Rather than smashing criminal drug gangs and reducing the availability of illicit substances, it has lined the pockets of criminals and increased drug use and all of its associated problems.[27] If you wanted to create a system that gives enormous power to drug cartels and criminal gangs, drug prohibition is the way to go. It has been a massive driver of crime across the world. The war on drugs has cost millions of lives and more than €1 trillion on enforcement that could have been spent on treatment and providing healthcare instead.

Illegal drugs are very harmful.

But most of the damage that illegal drugs cause in society does not come from the effects of the drugs themselves, but from the consequences of drug prohibition.

For a heroin addict, prohibition often means having to use and share dirty needles that transmit diseases. It means not knowing what is actually inside the drugs they buy. Drugs are cut with all sorts or more dangerous substances; for example heroin with fentanyl, which is cheaper but much more dangerous. Because of the illegality of drugs, it is very difficult for addicts to seek and receive help. Prohibition drives up the prices of drugs, meaning an addict has to find a lot of money. This means they often commit petty crimes and thefts. 70% of all shop thefts are related to drug addiction.[28] Most of these thefts would not occur, could the addict get a prescription of the drug from a doctor. Which is exactly what Britain had been doing up until the 1970s. A good book on the subject is 'Fierce Chemistry' by Harry Shapiro.

A book that outlines the disastrous effects of drug prohibition and explains its origins is 'Chasing the Scream' by Johann Hari. I recommend it.

In 'Good cop, bad war' Neil Wood explains the futility of the war on drugs from the perspective of an undercover cop infiltrating drug gangs. He describes how addicts need to actively recruit other addicts. Because drugs are so expensive, most addicts deal a little on the side to be able to afford them. They therefore constantly look for new people to sell them to. This mechanism makes drug addiction spread like a spider's web. It's something that simply wouldn't happen if addicts could get hold of their drugs through regulated ways.

Please refrain from giving me a moral lecture. From a purely moral point of view, there is absolutely nothing different between drinking a glass of whisky and having a line of coke. In both cases you are consuming a substance to alter your consciousness. The fact that there are drug cartels executing people in Colombia and drug gangs stabbing people in London has nothing to do with the cocaine itself, but is a consequence of prohibition. There are no alcohol cartels and no alcohol gangs, because alcohol is legal.

There were alcohol cartels and gangs, however, during alcohol prohibition in the US from 1920 to 1933. During this failed experiment, crime rates shot up and corruption in the police force increased.[29] At the same time, death rates from alcohol poisoning soared, because people started drinking all sorts of poisons. Around 30% fewer people drank, but for those who drank, the health consequences were much worse, as most of the alcohol available was cheaply produced and diluted with much worse chemicals, just as is the case now with illegal drugs.[30] One of the golden rules of drug prohibition is that the harshest substances will get consumed, as they are easier to smuggle. People stop drinking beer but drink the hard stuff instead. The same happens with drug prohibition.

Our understanding of drugs and addiction has moved past the point of idiotic slogans such as 'just say no' or the illusion that we can just get the world to stop taking drugs; and it's time for the government to act accordingly.

To understand what a devastating effect drug prohibition has, all one needs to do is to imagine what would happen if alcohol was made illegal tomorrow. A few might stop drinking, but most would continue to do so illegally. You could easily double the prison population by making alcohol illegal. Or you could reduce it with progressive drug legislation.

It does not have to be done all at once for all substances, but could be a gradual process.

Countries that have taken steps in the right direction have mostly seen positive outcomes. Since Portugal decriminalised drugs in 2001, drug deaths fell by 75%, HIV infections amongst users dropped massively and the overall crime rate in the country fell.[31] Uruguay has seen a decline in drug-related violence since it was the first country to legalise Cannabis in 2013.[32] Switzerland has brought its heroin problem under control in the early 90s when it introduced safe injection rooms, needle exchanges and methadone programs.[33]

Drugs are shit. They are terrible and they cause tremendous harm. I know this more than anyone and I will never touch a drug such as cocaine again in my life. I wouldn't even want to because it would do nothing for me. I'm past the age of clubbing and I came to understand where the inner pain came from that I needed to soothe so badly.

But I've seen too many people in prison for drug related offences not to realise that what we are doing at the moment is simply not working. We need a different approach.

Less Materialism

I was often struck by how obsessed many in prison were about money. The fancy clothes that some wore were a good example. I didn't get it. What was the point of wearing fancy clothes when you're in prison?

Our consumerist, ultra-capitalist society promises something that in reality, most of us will never be able to obtain. Especially those of us who come from disadvantaged communities. This creates frustration. In a world, where the richest 8 people own as much as the poorest half of the world population[34], most of us will simply not be able to obtain through legitimate means what we are told will make us happy. The resulting frustration might very well lead us to obtaining it through illegitimate means. After all, we're only taking what those at the top cheated us out of.

The neoliberal dog-eat-dog society we have created with its focus on competition, money, status and rugged individualism is a breeding ground for crime.[35]

The answer is to recognize how much neoliberalism has failed and try to create a world that is less materialistic and more about other values.

More Community and Belonging

We have created a world of alienation. Loneliness is an epidemic that now afflicts all age groups, even the very young. The connectedness that social media promised actually makes us more isolated, frustrated, insecure, afraid and angry. Social media makes us miserable and lonely.[36] We are constantly bombarded with images of perfect celebrities that will never be able to live up to; mostly because they are fictions and not real, but presented as real. All of this breeds resentment and has disastrous effects on mental health.

A sense of community in our towns and cities has broken down. As the role of the church declined, it has left a void. Very often, that void is filled by gangs.

We need to rebuild our communities and return a sense of belonging, rather than alienation.

Higher Priority to Mental Health Support

Mental health is everything, but it still not given enough importance in our society. If you want to receive help via the NHS, there is a long waiting list of many months just for simple counselling. If you need psychotherapy, you need to pay for it yourself. Fortunately, there are some low-cost services, such as TherapyHQ, which is the one I am using. Altogether, however, the service provided in society simply isn't enough by a long stretch.

Too much money is spent on fixing the symptoms of mental health issues later in life, rather than addressing the core issues early on. Not enough emphasis is given to prevention. Every young person should be able to access mental health support and use it from a very young age. This would prevent so much later damage in life and so many problems. Many crimes could be prevented with proper mental health support at the right age.

In order to have less prison, attitudes and perceptions need to change. When the government announces to build more prisons, the result should be public outcry. The questions to be asked should be: "Have we exhausted all other options? We should have less prison, not more. What can we do instead?"

When the government announces to make sentences harsher, the public should ask the government whether that's the best use of taxpayer's money rather than funding crime prevention programs in the community.

Prison should be seen as a necessary evil that we can't do without for the moment; and a rising prison population as a sign of failure. The public should understand that a future with less prison is a better future.

A RADICALLY DIFFERENT SYSTEM

It is the year 2040. We have created a better society.

The decisive moment came with the financial crash of 2028, when we did not repeat the mistakes we made in 2008, but held those responsible to account. We restructured and regulated not just the financial markets, but changed the entire economic model.

Due to automation many unskilled jobs were lost, which did not lead to ruin for many as feared, but actually made life better. Nobody now has to do mindless, repetitive jobs that make one sick mentally and physically.

We have introduced a Universal Basic Income, meaning everybody has enough money for the basics, and hardly anyone is homeless. We do have less money and work fewer hours, but are happier. Our values have changed completely. A sense of alienation and individualistic materialism has given way to more community and belonging. We value quality time over money and share a lot more. There are fewer millionaires, and billionaires don't exist. Super yachts and private jets are a thing of the past. The last luxury cruise company went bankrupt in 2032. There are significantly fewer cars, which are all electric.

The UK prison population has dropped from over 100,000 in the year 2028 to less than 20,000 today.

When people have addiction or mental health problems, they receive all the support they need in the community and do not go to prison. All drugs have been legalised. That does not mean that some people do not have addiction issues, but the criminality surrounding drugs has been eliminated, it is now mostly a health issue.

We have changed priorities in our criminal justice system. The government has pardoned all climate protesters that have been imprisoned and issued an apology, thanking them for their contribution towards saving our future. Hundreds of fossil fuel executives have been sentenced for their role in wilfully misleading the public and obfuscating the science for decades, leading to millions of unnecessary deaths.

Unfortunately, despite much progress, we still have no explanation or cure for psychopathology. Crime rates have dropped in certain areas, but crime still exists. Serial killers, terrorists, rapists and paedophiles still exist. Fraud still exists and people still try to cheat and take advantage. People still get angry, greedy, and jealous. People are still flawed and they still make stupid mistakes.

We have become much better at convicting those guilty of sexual crimes and domestic violence. In addition, due to improvements in society and better understanding and treatment of mental health issues early on, the actual number of these crimes has decreased. But they still exist, and in many cases there no other option than to lock someone away for the safety of the victim.

Whether you think this is most realistic vision of our future you've ever read, or a cloud-cuckoo-utopia is beside the point.

What I wanted to demonstrate is that crime and prison have everything to do with society, but very little with the individual. The humans in my scenario of 2040 are no different from the humans of today. It is society, however, that has changed.

We cannot change the fact that some people will always be evil, but we can change society. As soon as we change our priorities, we will have less crime and fewer people in prison. A society that cares about the environment, for example, will also need fewer prisons.

There is a reason that many environmental books have a chapter on prison. 'There's no planet B' by Tim Berners Lee is a good example; another is 'It's not that radical' by Mikaela Loach. Everything is connected. Prison is part of society, and how prisons are run tells you everything about the values of a society.

But rather than accepting this truth, we have been doing the opposite. We have not just kept prison hidden from sight; we have also pretended that prison is separate from society. We have used it as a dumping ground for everything that is too difficult for society to deal with, completely forgetting that it will bite us every time someone is released back into society. The people in prison aren't 'other people'. They are us.

But before I become too philosophical, let's look at what to do with the remaining 20,000 prisoners that we have in 2040. The reduction in the population has allowed us to build prisons in a completely different way and come up with a different system that we can create from the ground up.

One of the main flaws of the old system was that prison was the exact same for everyone, despite the fact that there are many different reasons why someone might have offended. Imagine a doctor who prescribes the exact same medicine to every single patient, regardless of whether they have a stomach ulcer or a dislocated shoulder.

Offenders are chucked into a cell for a few years without addressing the cause of their offending and then miraculously something is supposed to change. Sometimes it does, sometimes it doesn't. But when it does, it has nothing to do with the system.

The new system would therefore entirely focus on looking at the cause of the offending behaviour. The focus would be on trying to rehabilitate and provide opportunity for change.

There would be nine different categories of prisons. Only 4 would be in closed conditions, as only a percentage of the prison population are so dangerous they need to be locked away.

Closed conditions:

Psychopathology

Coercive behaviour (domestic violence, coercive control, stalking, rape, etc.)

Sexual deviance (paedophilia)

Terrorism, religious fanaticism & cult influence.

Open conditions:

Basic education (literacy; GCSE'S; A-levels)

Further education (apprenticeships & university degrees)

Vocational training (apprenticeships in trade – real qualifications)

Addiction & mental health (mostly in community)

Therapeutic community

50% of prisoners would therefore be in open conditions, compared to 5% in the current system. This would free up resources and staff to focus on rehabilitation.

Each prison type would be entirely focused on its specific purpose, staffed with experts. Prisoners would therefore know exactly why they are there and what they are trying to achieve during their sentence.

The same would be the case for officers. Officer training would be at least 2 years instead of the current 6 weeks. The first year would consist of general training and the second year of specialisation in any of the 9 types of prison.

The job of prison officer would be much more like social work or mental health worker, rather than simple turnkey.

The job would be a lot more interesting and challenging intellectually (The job of prison officer at the moment is incredibly challenging, but for all the wrong reasons).

Mental health support in the community will be much stronger, so mental health cases don't land in prison. Sounds expensive, I know, but nothing is as expensive as the prisons we have at the moment.

The breakdown of community leads to crime. We should work on giving young people a community again.

What could be the harm in trying something radically different? Especially considering that the current system couldn't possibly be worse than it is and cost more than any alternatives would cost.

EPILOGUE

Rehabilitation is possible. People can change. I have seen it many times during my time in prison and I can see it in myself. I've met many fellow inmates that I have done terrible things in the past that I would vouch for. They are simply not the same person anymore. Maybe they have learnt, maybe they have healed, and maybe they have simply grown older. In any case, they probably won't reoffend.

For some others I can't say the same thing. They haven't taken responsibility and have not grown. In many cases it might be because a broken system has let them down. In other cases, even a perfect system would have never been able to help them. But to declare them 'lost causes' and simply give up on improving the system would be defeatist.

Regardless of whether they can be rehabilitated or not, all prisoners are humans. The people I met in prison are no different from the people I meet today when I go to the gym, do my shopping or have a pint in a pub. Yes, they might be a more troubled, less educated, often lack manners and are frankly often quite annoying, but they are not a different species of human and they are not necessarily more 'evil'. There are many world leaders today and even some British politicians that I would without hesitation describe as more evil than most of the people I met in prison.

I am not the same person anymore that I was when I committed my offence. I have come to understand what went wrong in my life and why I made this horrible mistake. This understanding, unfortunately, has come at a huge price. The damage that I have caused is irreversible, and no amount of rehabilitation can change that. I am aware of that and I will forever be sorry.

Unfortunately, I can't change the past. But I can make people aware of how we could create a society that would have fewer victims of crime and fewer people in prison. People who call for prison reform are in fact good people who think about the damage that crime causes and think about the victims of crime. A better prison system will mean fewer victims of crime. A society with fewer people in prison will be a society that is better for everyone. Our goal should be to create a society where at some point in the future we simply won't need prisons.

The prison crisis has now opened a window. We now have the opportunity to explain why the system is broken. If the government does things well, it can explain to public that the system is broken exactly because too many have been sent to prison, whilst the prison system has been starved of funding, making rehabilitation impossible. Attention has been consistently diverted from the actual, societal causes of crime to seeing dumping criminals inside prison for ever longer as a solution.

Unfortunately, still not much of this seems to be happening. Most of the explanations still focus on simply not having built enough prison places. And Labour has pledged to build thousands more places over the coming years. Building more prison places is not the solution, but the problem.

Nevertheless, there are reasons to be hopeful. I am convinced that at least some positive changes will be made and that over time, public opinion will shift and politicians will be braver and more principled to make the right choices. Maybe we will actually see the 2040 that I have envisaged.

INFO BOXES INDEX

ENDNOTES

INTRODUCTION

1   https://www.independent.co.uk/news/uk/crime/prison-crisis-riots-overcrowding-early-dawn-b2598574.html
2   House of Commons Library, UK Prison Population Statistics (Georgina Sturge, 8th July 2024)
3   Office of National Statistics Centre for Crime and Justice, Crime in England and Wales: year ending June 2024
4   Institute for Crime and Policy Research, World Prison Population List , 14th edition (Helen Fair, Roy Walmsley, 2024)
5   https://thebulletin.org/2024/07/in-the-uk-a-dangerous-escalation-in-the-criminalization-of-climate-protests/
6   https://www.theguardian.com/environment/2024/dec/11/britain-leads-the-world-in-cracking-down-on-climate-activism-study-finds
7   https://www.globalwitness.org/en/press-releases/harsh-jail-time-climate-activists-threatens-democracy-and-climate-action/
8   https://www.theguardian.com/uk-news/article/2024/jul/31/how-false-online-claims-about-southport-knife-attack-spread-so-rapidly
9   https://www.express.co.uk/news/uk/2004051/exclusive-investigation-hundreds-jailed-southport-riots
10   https://www.independent.co.uk/news/uk/crime/southport-liverpool-merseyside-south-yorkshire-rotherham-b2617623 html
11   https://www.aljazeera.com/news/2024/9/6/uk-man-sentenced-to-nine-years-for-arson-after-far-right-riots
12   Prison Reform Trust, Bromley Briefings Prison Factfile (Winter 2022)
13   https://nij.ojp.gov/topics/articles/five-things-about-deterrence
14   https://www.statista.com/statistics/1100628/prison-sentence-length-in-england-and-wales-over-time/
15   https://vera-institute.files.svdcdn.com/production/downloads/publications/for-the-record-prison-paradox_02.pdf
16   https://www.standard.co.uk/news/crime/overcrowding-jails-prisons-violence-crime-chief-inspector-b1092389.html
17   HM Prison & Probation Service, Safety in Custody Statistics, England and Wales: Deaths in Prison Custody to September 2024 Assaults and Self-harm to June 2024 (31st Oct.'24)
18   https://www.instituteforgovernment.org.uk/publication/performance-tracker-2023/prisons

CHAPTER 1

1   House of Commons Library, Research Briefing, , The Prison Estate in England and Wales (Jacqueline Beard, 29th June '23)
2   https://victorian-prisons.com/about/victorian-prisons/
3   N. Morris, D.J. Rothman, The Oxford History of the Prison. The Practice of Punishment in Western Society (1997, Oxford University Press)
4   David Wilson, Pain and Retribution: A Short History of the English Prison, 1066 to the Present (Reaktion Books, 2014)
5   https://prisonreformtrust.org.uk/new-figures-reveal-scale-of-prison-capacity-crisis/
6   Howard League for Penal Reform, Revealed: The scale of prison overcrowding in England and Wales (1st August, 2019, www.howardleague.org)
7   https://victorian-prisons.com/about/victorian-prisons/
8   https://www.ucl.ac.uk/bentham-project/about-jeremy-bentham/panopticon
9   HM Inspectorate of Prisons, What happens to prisoners in a pandemic? A thematic review (February 2021, www.justiceinspectorates.gov.uk)
10   https://www.theguardian.com/commentisfree/2022/dec/07/public-life-matt-hancock-tories
11   HM Inspectorate of Prisons, What happens to prisoners in a pandemic? A thematic review (February 2021, www.justiceinspectorates.gov.uk)

12 HM Inspectorate of Prisons, HMP Wandsworth (Unannounced inspection, 22th April – 2th May 2024, www.justiceinspectorates.gov.uk)

13 https://lordslibrary.parliament.uk/coronavirus-the-challenge-for-prisons-and-offenders/; https://www.prisonersadvice.org.uk/information/pas-covid-19-response/

14 House of Commons Library, UK Prison Population Statistics (Georgina Sturge, 8th July 2024)

15 https://www.france24.com/en/20200427-as-france-releases-thousands-can-covid-19-end-chronic-prison-overcrowding

16 https://www.aljazeera.com/news/2020/4/14/turkey-to-free-one-third-of-its-prisoners-to-curb-coronavirus

17 HM Inspectorate of Prisons, What happens to prisoners in a pandemic? A thematic review (February 2021, www.justiceinspectorates.gov.uk)

18 T.Hewson, A.Shepherd, J.Hard, J.Shaw, Effects of the COVID-19 pandemic on the mental health of prisoners (The Lancet, July 2020)

19 Don Stemen, The Prison Paradox: More incarceration will not make us safer, (Loyola University Chicago, 2017); https://www.nao.org.uk/briefings/nao-briefing-comparing-international-criminal-justice-systems/

20 Denny, Meagan (2016) "Norway's Prison System: Investigating Recidivism and Reintegration," Bridges: A Journal of Student Research: Vol. 10 : Iss. 10 , Article 2.

21 L. Antenangeli, Ph.D., M. R. Durose, U.S. Department of Justice Office of Justice Programs Bureau of Justice Statistics, Recidivism of Prisoners Released in 24 States in 2008: A 10-Year Follow-Up Period (2008-2018) (Special Report, Sept. '21)

22 https://www.gov.uk/government/publications/sentencing-bill-2023

23 https://www.gov.uk/guidance/independent-sentencing-review-2024-to-2025

24 https://www.theguardian.com/society/2021/oct/05/short-jail-terms-fail-to-prevent-reoffending-says-former-england-and-wales-magistrate

25 https://www.politics.co.uk/news/2009/08/25/overcrowded-prisons-act-as-a-university-of-crime/

26 https://hmiprisons.justiceinspectorates.gov.uk/news/chief-inspectors-blog-drugs-and-disorder-worrying-times-for-prisons/

27 https://www.statista.com/statistics/1202172/cost-per-prisoner-england-and-wales/

28 Prison Reform Trust, Prison Reform Trust response to the Ministry of Justice consultation, Punishment and reform: effective community sentences

29 HM Prison & Probation Service, Offender Management Statistics Quarterly, October to December '23 (Published 25th April '24)

30 Prison Reform Trust, Bromley Briefings Prison Factfile (Winter 2022)

31 https://www.gov.uk/government/news/2000-extra-sitting-days-to-help-address-courts-crisis

32 HM Prison & Probation Service, Offender Management Statistics Quarterly, April to June'24 (Published 31st October '24)

33 Transform Justice, Presumed innocent but behind bars – is remand overused in England and Wales? (March 2018, www.transformjustice.org.uk)

34 Transform Justice, Presumed innocent but behind bars – is remand overused in England and Wales? (March 2018, www.transformjustice.org.uk)

35 https://www.theguardian.com/law/2024/dec/09/court-delays-driving-innocent-prisoners-to-plead-guilty-in-england-and-wales

36 House of Commons Justice Committee, Mental Health in prison (21st Sept. '21) https://committees.parliament.uk/publications/7455/documents/78054/default/

37 House of Commons Justice Committee, Mental Health in prison (21st Sept. '21) https://committees.parliament.uk/publications/7455/documents/78054/default/

38 HM Chief Inspector of Prisons for England and Wales, Annual Report 2021-2022

39 Dr. Graham Drucan, Centre for Mental Health, Prison Mental Health Services in England, 2023

40 Young S, Cocallis KM. Attention Deficit Hyperactivity Disorder (ADHD) in the Prison System. Current psychiatry reports. (2019 Jun 1;21(6):41.)

41 National Offender Management Service, Working with offenders with personality disorder (Second edition, Feb. 2014)

42 NICE, 'Mental health of adults in contact with the criminal justice system: identification and management of mental health problems and integration of care for adults in contact with the criminal justice system', (November 2014

43 HM Prison & Probation Service, Safety in Custody Statistics, England and Wales: Deaths in Prison Custody to September 2024 Assaults and Self-harm to June 2024 (31st Oct.'24)

44 https://prisonreformtrust.org.uk/self-harm-and-suicide-rising-as-prisons-struggle-to-meet-mental-health-need/

45 https://www.spectator.co.uk/article/too-many-people-are-being-recalled-to-prison/

46 Ibid.

47 Ibid.

48 https://www.prisonadvice.org.uk/latest/news/new-figures-show-a-44-increase-in-prison-recalls/

49 Ibid.

50 Ibid.

51 https://www.bbc.co.uk/sounds/play/m0024419
52 https://revolving-doors.org.uk/recalls-in-crisis-what-needs-to-change/
53 https://www.theguardian.com/uk/2006/nov/13/prisonsandprobation.topstories3
54 David Wilson, Pain and Retribution: A Short History of the English Prison, 1066 to the Present (Reaktion Books, 2014)
55 https://www.theguardian.com/commentisfree/2015/mar/25/strangeways-1990-prison-riot-inhumane-conditions
56 N. Morris, D.J. Rothman, The Oxford History of the Prison. The Practice of Punishment in Western Society (1997, Oxford University Press)

CHAPTER 2

1 https://www.theguardian.com/society/2020/feb/13/psychoactive-drugs-linked-ambulance-callouts-prison-hmp-wealstun-spice
2 https://gdpo.swan.ac.uk/?p=538
3 https://www.shannontrust.org.uk/stories/one-way-to-level-up-is-to-ensure-that-nobody-is-left-out-of-learning
4 https://www.nber.org/system/files/working_papers/w15945/w15945.pdf
5 https://www.thoughtco.com/biological-determinism-4585195
6 Mobius, Markus M. and Tanya S. Rosenblat. Why beauty matters. (American Economic Review 96, no. 1: 222-235,2006)
7 CJ McKinney, M.Gower, Research Briefing, House of Commons Library, Deportation of foreign national offenders (2nd Aug. '24)

CHAPTER 3

1 https://www.legislation.gov.uk/uksi/1999/728/made
2 https://www.publicsectorcatering.co.uk/news/prison-food-budget-increases-25-202324
3 S.Goudi, R.Tobi, The Food Foundation, The Broken Plate 2023: Technical Report (June 2023)
4 https://www.stwater.co.uk/news/news-releases/a-sentence-for-flushing-food-down-the-loo-/
5 Gesch, C.B., Hammond, S.M., Hampson, S.E., Eves, A., Crowder, M.J.
   Influence of supplementary vitamins, minerals and essential fatty acids on the antisocial behaviour of young adult prisoners. Randomised, placebo-controlled trial. (British Journal of Psychiatry, 2002, 181, 22-8.)
6 https://www.england.nhs.uk/blog/reducing-healthcare-inequalities-for-those-in-contact-with-the-criminal-justice-system/
7 US Department of Justice, Bureau of Justice Statistics, Survey of prison inmates, 2016, Medical Problems Reported by Prisoners (June 2021)
8 www.foodbehindbars.co.uk
9 David Wilson, Pain and Retribution: A Short History of the English Prison, 1066 to the Present (Reaktion Books, 2014)
10 Ibid.
11 N. Morris, D.J. Rothman, The Oxford History of the Prison. The Practice of Punishment in Western Society (1997, Oxford University Press)
12 https://prisonreformtrust.org.uk/wp-content/uploads/1991/02/Woolf-report-summary-of-findings.pdf
13 N. Morris, D.J. Rothman, The Oxford History of the Prison. The Practice of Punishment in Western Society (1997, Oxford University Press)
14 https://www.poauk.org.uk/news-events/news-room/posts/2022/january/national-chair-the-service-is-speeding-towards-a-major-staffing-crisis-and-the-government-refuses-to-listen/

CHAPTER 4

1 Jeffrey Archer, *A Prison Diary- Volume 1: Hell*, (2003, Pan)

CHAPTER 6

1   https://www.healthline.com/nutrition/12-benefits-of-meditation
2   https://www.theppt.org.uk/about-us/

CHAPTER 7

1   https://www.crestadvisory.com/post/rewiring-justice-to-transform-punishment-rehabilitation-for-
    the-21st-century
2   R. Allen, Crime and Justice Studies, What does the Public think about Prison? (2002) https://www.
    crimeandjustice.org.uk/sites/crimeandjustice.org.uk/files/09627250208553484.pdf
3   https://yougov.co.uk/politics/articles/41641-criminal-sentencing-too-soft-say-two-thirds-briton
4   Prison Reform Trust, The Bromley Prison Factfile (Winter 2022)
5   Ibid.
6   https://www.independent.co.uk/news/uk/home-news/prison-crisis-violence-drugs-justice-
    b2586304.html
7   https://hmiprisons.justiceinspectorates.gov.uk/news/chief-inspectors-blog-drugs-and-disorder-
    worrying-times-for-prisons/
8   HM Prison & Probation Service, Safety in Custody Statistics, England and Wales: Deaths in Prison
    Custody to September 2024 Assaults and Self-harm to June 2024 (31st Oct.'24)
9   HM Prison & Probation Service, Safety in Custody Statistics, England and Wales: Deaths in Prison
    Custody to September 2024 Assaults and Self-harm to June 2024 (31st Oct.'24)
10 https://happiful.com/what-is-mean-world-syndrome
11 https://www.ipsos.com/en-uk/ipsos-trust-in-professions-veracity-index-2023
12 https://labour.org.uk/updates/stories/labour-party-prisons-policy-how-we-will-fix-the-prisons-
    crisis-and-keep-criminals-behind-bars/

CHAPTER 8

8   https://www.youtube.com/watch?v=p2aMRJPFPd8

CHAPTER 9

1   David Wilson, Pain and Retribution: A Short History of the English Prison, 1066 to the Present
    (Reaktion Books, 2014)
2   N. Morris, D.J. Rothman, The Oxford History of the Prison. The Practice of Punishment in Western
    Society (1997, Oxford University Press)
3   https://www.prisonstudies.org/country/united-states-america
4   https://www.gov.uk/guidance/independent-sentencing-review-2024-to-2025
5   https://www.lbc.co.uk/news/james-timpson-only-third-prisoners-behind-bars-starmer/
6   https://theconversation.com/new-scorecards-show-under-1-of-reported-rapes-lead-to-convic-
    tion-criminologist-explains-why-englands-justice-system-continues-to-fail-180345
7   https://www.theguardian.com/law/2024/dec/06/trials-collapse-as-victims-abandon-cases-amid-
    long-court-delays
8   HM Prison & Probation Service, Offender Management Statistics Quarterly, April to June'24 (Pub-
    lished 31st October '24)
9   Transform Justice, Presumed innocent but behind bars – is remand overused in England and Wales?
    (March 2018, www.transformjustice.org.uk)
10 HM Prison & Probation Service, Offender Management Statistics Quarterly, April to June'24 (Pub-
    lished 31st October '24)
11 https://www.prisonadvice.org.uk/latest/news/new-figures-show-a-44-increase-in-prison-recalls/

12 https://www.prisonersadvice.org.uk/information/pas-articles-key-cases-responses/unlawful-recall-case-significance/
13 https://www.crestadvisory.com/post/community-sentences-where-did-it-all-go-wrong
14 https://www.transformjustice.org.uk/focus-areas/resolving-crime-out-of-court/
15 https://www.westmidlands-pcc.gov.uk/lives-changed-by-offender-to-rehab-scheme/
16 https://howardleague.org/blog/why-short-prison-sentences-must-go/
17 https://commonslibrary.parliament.uk/research-briefings/sn06086/
18 https://socialistworker.co.uk/news/more-activists-jailed-for-speaking-about-the-climate-crisis-in-court/
19 https://www.theguardian.com/environment/2024/dec/20/just-stop-oil-activist-jail-christmas
20 https://www.theguardian.com/environment/2024/dec/11/britain-leads-the-world-in-cracking-down-on-climate-activism-study-finds
21 https://www.thetimes.com/article/cameron-sickened-by-prisoner-vote-j3zf67bbm2t
22 https://equalitytrust.org.uk/violence/
23 https://worldpopulationreview.com/country-rankings/crime-rate-by-country
24 https://worldpopulationreview.com/country-rankings/gini-coefficient-by-country
25 http://www.bignam.org/Publications/BIG_Assessment_report_08b.pdf
26 https://www.nacro.org.uk/news/newly-released-government-data-reveals-that-two-thirds-of-people-who-are-released-from-prison-homeless-reoffend-within-a-year/
27 https://civilrights.org/edfund/resource/the-war-on-drugs-has-failed-commission-says/
28 https://publications.parliament.uk/pa/cm5802/cmselect/cmhaff/141/14108.htm
29 https://www.cato.org/policy-analysis/alcohol-prohibition-was-failure
30 https://www.pbs.org/kenburns/prohibition/unintended-consequences
31 https://transformdrugs.org/blog/drug-decriminalisation-in-portugal-setting-the-record-straight
32 https://www.newstimes.com/news/article/Uruguay-Legalized-Marijuana-and-the-Crime-Rate-12555837.php
33 https://transformdrugs.org/blog/heroin-assisted-treatment-in-switzerland-successfully-regulating-the-supply-and-use-of-a-high-risk-injectable-drug
34 https://www.oxfam.org/en/press-releases/just-8-men-own-same-wealth-half-world
35 https://www.theguardian.com/politics/2005/nov/24/ukcrime.uk
36 Jonathan Haidt, The Anxious Generation: How the Great Rewiring of Childhood is Causing an Epidemic of Mental Illness (Penguin, 2024)

www.ingramcontent.com/pod-product-compliance
Lightning Source LLC
LaVergne TN
LVHW091258080426
835510LV00007B/309